THE GREEKS

HOW THEY LIVE AND WORK

The Greeks

HOW THEY LIVE AND WORK

T. R. B. Dicks

PRAEGER PUBLISHERS
New York . Washington

BOOKS THAT MATTER

Published in the United States of America in 1971
by Praeger Publishers, Inc.
111 Fourth Avenue, New York, N.Y. 10003

Library of Congress Catalog Card Number : 74 – 165843

Printed in Great Britain

Contents

List of Illustrations

(The photographs not otherwise acknowledged are from the author's collection)

To my mother and to the memory of my father

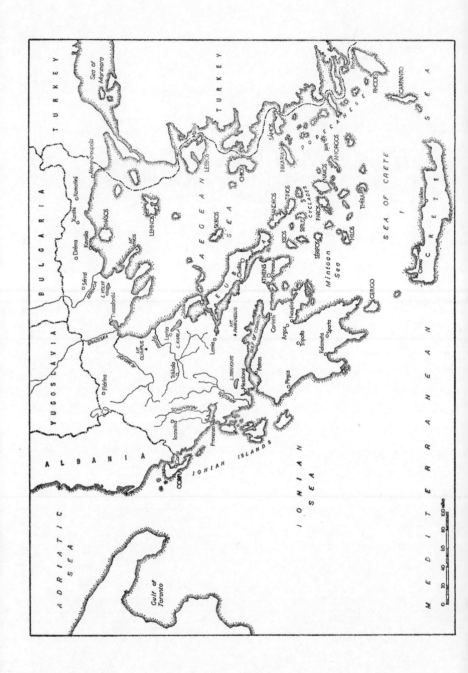

Introductory Note

A BOOK dealing largely with the contemporary way of life of the Greeks needs a brief introductory note. Since 21 April 1967 Greece has been ruled by a military junta, a fact that has made the writing of certain sections of this book difficult. The difficulty has concerned the availability of reliable, unbiased information on the colonels' régime and, in particular, the reconciling of contradictory views and attitudes which reflect either support or condemnation of the present situation.

The military *coup* came as a shock to international opinion, except to those who had a knowledge of modern Greek history, and to many of the Greeks themselves who had long seen military dictatorship as a conceivable, even probable, turn of events. That democracy is not allowed in the very country from which it sprang has been the cry of many lovers of Greece, but it is debatable whether true democracy has ever existed in Greece from the time of its liberation in the nineteenth century. In the western world extensive campaigns have been directed against the Greek régime and anti-government propaganda has been spread by many influential persons. The conflicting reports are perhaps best illustrated over the question of the detention of political prisoners and their alleged torture, where it has been extremely difficult to distinguish fact from propaganda. Equally, the state of the country's economy has been the subject of mixed reports. The view that Greece has witnessed a grave economic setback since 1967 is certainly not supported by UN and OECD reports or by other recent surveys. It may well prove that the measures taken by the colonels to build a permanent power structure will prove extremely beneficial in terms of the country's economic development.

Yet there is another side of the régime which appears anything but favourable. The colonels still lack a stable base of domestic support which would enable them to function freely and this has meant the need for repression in many fields of activity. It began as a comic opera when a ban was announced on beards and long hair for men, and on mini-skirts for women, tourists included. But army orders to the civilian population reached graver proportions in press censorship and the control of the education system and of all mass media. These and similar measures have had far-reaching implications for the nation.

This book is an attempt to convey to the reader the main characteristics and problems current in contemporary Greek life. The political question is, of course, paramount, but the effects of the disruption of normal political life on the mass of the population is still not known, especially in rural areas. Some of the pertinent aspects of Greek politics are discussed in Chapter 3, but no attempt has been made to take sides for or against the present régime, largely because it would destroy the very purpose of this book. A number of books are in print dealing with this issue that has rocked the allegiances of the western world.

I

The Country and the People

THE term 'Greece' has assumed a variety of meanings throughout the course of history and has not been used to describe a
fixed geographical entity. The modern country covers an area
of 50,168 square miles and is almost equivalent in size to
England alone or the state of Alabama. Of this total area the
mainland covers 40,328 square miles and the islands, including
Crete, the remaining 9,840 square miles. In the north Greece
is bounded by the continental mass of Balkan Europe and has a
frontier of 500 miles with the countries of Albania, Yugoslavia,
Bulgaria and Turkey. Part of this frontier follows the Rhodope
massif and the Gramos-Vitsi ranges, and eastwards the Evros
river marks the boundary with Turkey. In addition to land
frontiers there are 9,375 miles of coastline bordering the Ionian
Sea in the west, the Aegean in the east, and the Sea of Crete and
the eastern basin of the Mediterranean in the south. The eastern
sea boundary with Turkey is complex but lies close to the shores
of Anatolia, so that the majority of the Aegean islands lie within
Greek territory.

The modern state owes its existence to the period after 1830
when, following the War of Independence, which commanded
wide sympathy through the western world, Greece broke away
from Ottoman rule and full autonomy was established. The
territory of early nineteenth-century Greece coincided with the
area of 'traditional Greece,' a designation implying the tip of the
Balkan peninsula south of the Gulfs of Arta and Volos and including the islands of Euboea and the central Aegean. This area

is typically Mediterranean in climate and general way of life, and historically it formed the heart of classical Greece.

Greece: generalised relief map

During the nineteenth century, and particularly since 1913, boundary extensions northwards acquired a large appendage which is often termed 'New Greece.' This area, transitional between the Mediterranean proper and the continental Balkan interior, was regarded in ancient times as Hellenised rather than truly Greek in character. The contemporary development of the country, however, has erased any significant cultural differences which might have existed during the earlier decades of this century.

A third concept of Greece, although falling outside the scope of this book, should be mentioned. It refers to the Greek communities overseas or the Greeks of the dispersal. In the course of twenty-seven centuries the Greeks, compelled by the inherent poverty of their environment and lured by better prospects elsewhere, have emigrated in large numbers. As early as 750BC trading colonies were established around the Mediterranean and Black Sea coasts, and later the conquests of Alexander the Great resulted in Hellenic influence being extended to cover much of the Middle East. The presence of substantial Greek communities in western Anatolia during the early part of this century presented great economic and political problems to both Turkish and Greek governments. Emigration has continued to the present time and it is estimated that there are about half as many Greeks domiciled abroad as there are living in Greece. Expatriate Greeks remain a powerful source of moral and financial influence on the country as a whole.

PHYSICAL CHARACTERISTICS

It has often been said that 'Greece is a land of the mountains and the sea.' Great areas of the country are over 3,000ft and many summits reach 6,000ft. The highest mountain, Olympus, the traditional home of the gods, rises to 9,550ft. The mountains stretch out as peninsulas which, in many cases, are continued into the Aegean as chains of islands. Gulfs and bays penetrate far inland, and few places in Greece are more than 50 miles from the coast. The coastal plain is usually narrow, but there are also numerous upland plains in the interior which have formed regions of settlement from earliest times.

Geologically the country consists of old blocks of resistant rocks occupying the north-eastern part of Greece and the central Aegean islands, and a series of younger and weaker rocks, folded during the Tertiary earth movements, occupying western and southern Greece. Recent uplift and fracturing has affected both zones and this has continued to the present time as the incidence of earthquakes indicate. The Aegean itself owes its very existence to recent faulting, as do the gulfs of Corinth and Patras which separate the Peloponnesus from the northern mainland. The presence of hot springs and a line of volcanic peaks stretching from the dormant cone of Methana in the Saronic Gulf, through

Milos and Thera to Kos, provide further evidence of instability. The Kaimeni islands, rising in the centre of the explosion crater of Thera, are the new cones of a still active volcano. The most destructive earthquakes which have occurred during recent years took place in the Ionian islands of Cephalonia, Zante and Ithaca in 1953, in the Magnesia district of Thessaly in 1955 and in the island of Thera in 1956.

The most important natural feature of the country is a series of high mountain ranges (the Pindus) which extends southwards from Albania and Yugoslavia as an extension of the Dinaric Alps. This mountainous backbone of the Greek mainland is composed predominantly of limestone which gives rise to extensive areas of *karst* (eroded limestone) scenery with innumerable sink-holes, underground streams and bare waterless localities. The rugged, inhospitable landscape has been intensified by recent faulting which has produced steep slopes, escarpments and deep ravines. The Pindus, therefore, provides a most effective barrier to communications between east and west, and astride it the country's main geographical and historical regions have evolved.

To the west of the main Pindus range, in Epirus and Acarnania, a series of longitudinal valleys and ranges lie parallel to the coast and make access inland difficult. To the east a number of mountainous appendages of the main range extend in a south-westerly direction, giving rise to rugged promontories which are continued into the Aegean as island chains. The large and elongated island of Euboea, together with Andros, Tinos and Myconos, is a structural continuation of the highlands of central Greece. The Cycladic islands are exposed summits of the prolongation of highlands in Boeotia and Attica and demonstrate the structural links between the Greek mainland and Asia Minor.

To the south of the gulfs of Corinth and Patras the Pindus is continued as the wild and rugged limestone highlands of the Peloponnesus. From the central mountainous core of Arcadia the main chain can be traced southwards to the island of Cythera and then through Crete, Karpathos and Rhodes into Asia

Minor. Structurally Crete forms the southern mountainous rim of the Aegean basin.

The lowland element in the Greek landscape is not very considerable, but it has naturally played a very important role in the life of the country. Most of the coastal plains and interior basins were formed during the faulting of late Tertiary times, and in southern and western Greece they tend to be discontinuous and isolated features. The major plains are found in the north and east, of which the Plain of Thessaly is by far the most extensive and quite exceptional. In Macedonia and Thrace river basins and alluvial lowlands are extensive, and these are separated by mountainous blocks of a very complex geological history. It is significant that today Macedonia and Thessaly are the country's most advanced agricultural regions. Here the more extensive lowlands have aided progress in mechanisation and scientific farming.

CLIMATE

Although Greece is generally regarded as a Mediterranean country, its climate is of a transitional character, with features of the continental climate of eastern Europe as well as the distinguishing marks of the Mediterranean régime. The distribution of mountains and lowlands and the indented nature of the coastline emphasise strongly the effect of location on climate. On the one hand the mountainous character of much of the country carries continental conditions as far south as the central Peloponnesus; on the other the numerous bays and gulfs allow the influences of the Mediterranean Sea to penetrate in places far into the highlands. The result of both these controls is seen in the great variety of local climates. In general terms, however, the interior of northern and central Greece, and to a lesser extent the Peloponnesian highlands, can be said to experience a continental climate where snow is common in winter, and the remainder of the country, southern Greece and the islands, share the Mediterranean characteristics.

B

In winter a low-pressure system is situated over much of the country and a series of depressions moving eastwards brings rain, particularly to the western coasts. The reverse situation is true in summer when a high-pressure system dominates, bringing hot, sunny weather with very little rain. A series of steady north winds over the eastern basin of the Mediterranean is common in summer; these winds were known to the ancient Greeks as the Etesians.

Most of the country's rainfall is associated with the winter cyclonic influences. Summer rainfall, apart from thunderstorms, is slight and much of southern Greece and the Aegean islands experience the true Mediterranean régime with a winter rainfall maximum in November, December and January and an almost rainless summer. The average rainfall total for the three summer months, June, July and August, for the towns of Patras, Nauplion and Kalamata is around 0.9in. In northern Greece there is a slight autumn and spring maximum and the summer drought is less well defined. In general terms annual rainfall totals diminish from west to east and from north to south, but there are many local variations. The December figures for the Ionian islands of Corfu (7.8in) and Zante (9.2in) stand in marked contrast to those recorded at eastern stations, for example, Athens (2.6in), Chalkis (2.8in), Volos (2.1in) and Nauplion (3.6in). The west coast has an average annual rainfall of around 43in compared with 20in for the east coast. There is, however, especially in summer, a marked increase in rainfall totals with altitude.

Temperatures are not generally extreme. The winter cold, except in the mountains, is modified by coastal influences and the heat of summer is tempered by sea breezes and the northerly winds. Sudden changes, however, can occur from day to day and the accentuated local relief causes great irregularities from place to place. In broad terms the temperature of Greece shows an increase from north to south, but this simple latitudinal pattern is considerably modified by altitude. January is usually the coldest month and the lowest temperatures occur in the upland basins of the Pindus mountains. Kozani has an average January temperature of 35°F, Trikkala 41°F, Larisa 42°F and Salonica 42°F. Maximum temperatures occur in late July or early August when much of the country can experience over 80°F. At Larisa and Kalamata 113° has been recorded, 114°F at Iraklion in Crete, and 116°F at Tripolis in the central Peloponnesus. These figures, of course, are exceptions rather than the general rule.

VEGETATION

Southern Greece has a typical Mediterranean vegetation where trees, shrubs and small plants are adapted to withstand the summer drought. Oak, laurel, oleander and juniper are common species, together with conifers such as the cypress and Aleppo pine. Many smaller species have a winter and spring growing period and a summer resting period. Spring is a strikingly colourful season, where by the end of April cyclamens, anemones, poppies, mimosa, wistaria and a host of fruit trees blossom in profusion. The contrast between spring and summer is most striking in Attica and the Aegean islands, the latter season producing a sun-parched landscape.

In the highlands of southern Greece and at lower altitudes in the north the character of the vegetation changes as summer rainfall and winter cold increase. Deciduous oak, chestnut and beech on the lower and middle slopes grade into conifers at higher altitudes, and above the tree line alpine pastures or rock flora predominate. Human activity as well as natural factors has greatly modified the vegetation cover. Centuries of burning, over-grazing and general mismanagement have stripped much of Greece of its original vegetation cover. The direct result of this over-exploitation has led to the secondary growth of a dense tangle of thorny undergrowth known as *maquis*. This is a mixed plant community where one species rarely dominates. Re-afforestation is now practised in Greece and much progress has been accomplished through external financial aid. This is obviously a long-term development and the main physical difficulties are related to climate, inaccessibility and exhausted soils.

THE GREEK PEOPLE

Geographical position is an important aspect of a country's total environment. Greece stands at the crossroads between Europe, Africa and Asia, on land as well as on sea, and this has had an important bearing on its historical and contemporary development and on the ethnic origins of its people. Throughout the course of history geographical position has occasionally conferred privileges on Greece, but all too frequently it has brought calamity.

Strong links bind the present state with the distant past, and the complicated history of the Greeks sheds light on certain aspects of their character. The land they now inhabit includes the sites where the ancient Cretan-Cycladic or Minoan civilisation of the third and second millennia BC flourished. Sir Arthur Evans' discovery of the vast palace at Knossos, Crete, with its intricate ground plan, substantiated the ancient tradition that Crete was a mighty sea empire whose civilisation spread to the Greek mainland and over the Aegean world. The peoples who occupied Knossos and other Cretan cities, such as Mallia and Phaestos, belonged to the short, dark Mediterranean type and were distinct from the taller Illyrian peoples of the Balkan interior.

The progenitors of the Greeks and the Greek language, however, were the Achaean peoples of Indo-European origin. Around the year 2000BC they entered as colonists from the north and gradually extended their influence south into the peninsula. The Achaeans soon entered into relations with the Cretans and developed a form of civilisation closely resembling the Minoan. This was the Mycenaean civilisation, named after its type site, Mycenae, in the Argolid. By 1400BC, following the decline of Crete, Mycenae and the Greek mainland took over the leadership of the Aegean world. Our knowledge of the Achaean period stems mainly from the great discoveries of Schliemann, who again corroborated—in some cases to an astonishing degree—the general reliability of tradition and legend. Homer's 'Golden Mycenae' became a reality, and excavations at Troy on the coast of Asia Minor revealed a civilisation remarkably similar to that described in the *Iliad*. Prior to the great discoveries on Crete and at Mycenae it was generally assumed that Greek history began in 776BC, the traditional date of the first Olympic Games. Everything before that date was regarded as belonging to the realms of myth and legend, created by the Greeks in order to fill in the blanks in their unknown past.

The rich urban and commercial civilisation established by the Mycenaeans came to an end around 1100BC when new influxes of Dorians came into the north from Macedonia. Also of Indo-European origin, they colonised areas as far south as the Peloponnesus where they founded Sparta, but it appears they were a less civilised people and life reverted to a more primitive existence. Considerable population displacement accompanied the Dorian movement, but towards the close of antiquity a more or less single homogeneous cultural entity had formed which remained little modified for a number of centuries.

From the beginning of the fourth century AD onwards, new ethnic groups appeared in Greece. The Goths entered from the north as a series of raiding parties and in their wake came Avars and hordes of Slavs, whose raiding towards the end of the sixth century began to pass into settlement. Slavic settlement became so widespread that the interior of the Greek peninsula came to be known as *Sclavinia*. The strength of Hellenism, however, is seen in the way these new invading groups were quickly assimilated linguistically and culturally by the Greeks. Later ethnic elements included the Turks, Vlachs, Armenians and colonies of Albanians.

Today Greece is inhabited by a remarkably homogeneous and fundamentally Greek cultural group. The only minorities are small numbers of Jews, Vlachs, Albanians and Turks, who in total amount to no more than 6 per cent of the population. It would be incorrect to assume, however, that the modern

Greek conforms to one uniform physical type; since the early nineteenth century racial elements have entered Greece from almost every country in the eastern Mediterranean and the Middle East. It is important to realise that Greek nationality today is determined primarily by religion and language; the former Greek Orthodoxy, and the latter a direct legacy of ancient Greece.

CHIEF HISTORICAL LANDMARKS

The movement southwards into Greece of the Dorian peoples lasted a number of centuries and the resulting unsettled conditions were unfavourable to material advance. Between 1100 and 800BC Greece entered a period known as the Dark Age, a designation which is apt in two senses. In the first place the period is obscure since the complete breakdown with the east makes it difficult to date any remains with precision, and secondly, according to many scholars, it was a time of great impoverishment and little artistic development. The Mycenaean organisation, as noted by Homer, was one of tribal areas ruled by kings or chieftains who held regular council under the presidency of Agamemnon, a kind of feudal overload. By 800BC, when the curtain rises again after the Dark Age, a completely new system of political organisation appears. Southern Greece is now divided into a number of independent political units known as *poleis* (singular *polis*) or city states, each with its own system of government, its industry and commerce. Notable among the great cities of the mainland were Athens, Corinth, Thebes, Sparta and Sicyon. In terms of area the city states were small, and varied from about 120 square miles in the case of Doris to larger states such as Athens which controlled 1,000 square miles. A combination of population increase, leading to land hunger, and internal strife and political discontent occasioned emigration and the foundation of colonies around the shores of the Mediterranean and Black Seas. This can be regarded as the first great period of Greek migration.

Although the Greeks were very conscious of their common nationhood, which found expression in such great gatherings as the Olympic Games, political unity was never achieved and the history of Greek inter-state relations is largely the history of rival powers in search of security, both economic and military. Ultimately it became a rivalry of the most powerful cities, Athens, Sparta and for a time Thebes. The Peloponnesian War between Athens and Sparta, which began in 431BC and continued for twenty-seven years, reveals the magnitude of these rivalries.

The internal strife of the city states paved the way for their own decline, and in Macedonia a new power was to emerge. Under Philip of Macedon, and particularly as a result of the conquests of his son, Alexander, between 334 and 323BC, Hellenism spread to Anatolia, Syria, Egypt, Persia and even as far as the Punjab. The Macedonian Empire maintained its dominance in Greece until 167BC when warfare and defeat resulted in Greece gradually being absorbed into the Roman Empire.

The prestige of Greek civilisation was such that the Romans not only left the Greeks to the enjoyment of their municipal liberties, but also sent their sons to attend the Greek schools of art and literature. Athens continued to be a great intellectual centre to which men came from all parts of the empire. In AD324, when the Roman Empire for the purposes of administrative convenience was subdivided into two, the Western and the Eastern, the Emperor Constantine chose the ancient city of Byzantium on the Bosphorus as the capital of the new Christian Empire of the East. Byzantium was enlarged to form the city of 'New Rome' (Constantinople) and the Roman Empire of the East continued for centuries as a permanent factor amidst the changing political fortunes of Europe and the east. While Rome was tottering under the repeated blows of the Goths, Vandals and Huns, the Eastern Empire consolidated its control over most of the Balkan peninsula, Asia Minor, Cyprus and other parts of the Middle East. In culture the empire was characterised by Greek and Roman traditions. In language, literature and theology Greek influence was paramount; in law, diplomacy and military tradition it relied on Roman experience.

But although Greek culture became an important element in Byzantine civilisation the imperial city grew at the expense of Greece. Constantinople, rather than Athens, became the important factor in Greek life, and Greece became increasingly provincial. The Greeks themselves now became known, not as 'Hellenes', but as 'Romaioi'. The Emperor Justinian, in 529, virtually abolished the University of Athens, the stronghold of pagan philosophy, and it was northern Greece, under the leadership of Salonica, that was to prosper from Byzantine rule. Yet of all the empires that have ruled Greece it is Byzantium that has left the most lasting mark on contemporary Greek culture in the form of the Orthodox Church. Many Greeks still think of Constantinople as the 'capital,' and the dream of regaining the city has strongly coloured political thinking this century.

The culturally and economically rich empire came to an end when the Ottoman Turks captured Constantinople in 1453. Within a few years Turkish rule spread over Greece and the whole Balkan peninsula. For Greece this marked a period of oppression and cultural extinction, although the Turks allowed Christian life to continue and the bishops and priests were invested with judicial as well as spiritual rights. Gradually, however, the position of the Greeks under Ottoman rule improved and some were entrusted by the Sultan with diplomatic functions. Towards the close of the Ottoman period the Greeks also had most of the commerce and shipping in their hands and their economic dominance was greatest in Constantinople and in other large commercial centres of the Ottoman Empire: Salonica, Smyrna, Alexandria and Adrianople. The traditional Ottoman disdain of mercantile activities enabled the Greeks and other minority groups virtually to monopolise business life.

The history of the medieval-Turkish period is complicated by the appearance of European powers who gained territorial possessions and trading rights in the Greek peninsula and islands. Notable among these were the Venetians, whose influence was marked in the Ionian Isles, Crete and the Cyclades. Franks, Genoese and Crusaders also belong to this period. Many of these occupations formed curious episodes in the history of Greece

and they have left many traces upon the countryside. Venice
in particular played a major role in the defence of the Aegean
against the Turk, and the island of Tinos lingered on under
Venetian sovereignty until as late as 1715.

In 1821 the Greeks revolted against their Turkish masters in
a war that was to last many years. Officially no state would
give them help, but the struggle for freedom was supported by
volunteers from all parts of the world, among them the British
Admiral Cochrane who organised the Greek navy, and the poet
Byron who died in the cause at Mesolongi. Britain, France
and Russia undertook to mediate between Greece and Turkey,
but the decisive victory came in 1827 when the Turkish fleet
was annihilated at Navarino by a fleet of the three powers.

A new Greek kingdom was constituted in 1830, but it was a
small country and nine-tenths of the Greek population of the
Balkans were still left in Ottoman lands. Utterly devastated after
the war, the kingdom was not even the centre of the Greek
world. It included no city of any importance within its boundaries and its cultural, economic and religious centres were all
abroad. Constantinople was the centre of the Greek bourgeoisie
and, although Athens was proclaimed capital, in no way could
it compete with the national and cultural prestige of the Turkish
city. In large part, therefore, the story of independent Greece
is one of political and military strategies which resulted in the
liberation and acquisition of those Greek-inhabited regions that
initially remained under Turkish rule. To many Greeks this
became a dream of rebuilding the Byzantine Empire, a conception which came to be called the 'Great Idea'.

In 1864, as a gesture of friendliness, Britain ceded to Greece
the Ionian Islands, which had been a British protectorate since
1851. By the Congress of Berlin in 1878 Greece gained Thessaly
and part of Epirus. The 1912 Balkan War, in which Greece,
Bulgaria, Serbia and Montenegro formed an alliance against
the Turks, resulted in Epirus and part of Macedonia, including
Salonica, being annexed to Greece, as well as the islands of
Mytilene, Chios and Samos, together with Crete. The Dodecanese would also have been included but for the fact that they had

been occupied by Italy as the result of her war with Turkey two years earlier. Bulgaria, unsatisfied with her share of the liberated territories, was defeated by her former allies in the short campaign known as the Second Balkan War (1913).

By the Treaty of Sèvres (1920), which followed World War I, Greece came near to the realisation of her national claims with the acquisition of the whole of Thrace and the Smyrna district of Asia Minor. In 1922 the Turkish nationalist movement, led by Kemal Ataturk, regained the former Turkish territories, and the consequence of the Greek defeat was the expulsion of all the Greeks from Asia Minor and Thrace. For centuries there had

Growth of the Greek State

been flourishing Greek towns in these provinces, and one and a half million Greeks found themselves evicted in exchange for around 390,000 Turks living in Greece. The transfer of population was supervised by the Convention of Lausanne and only slowly, and mainly with the help of international relief organisations, did Greece recover from the acute economic and social burden. The conception of a 'Greater Greece,' which was the main ideological and political slogan throughout the nineteenth and early twentieth centuries, was squashed. The Asia Minor disaster led to the Treaty of Lausanne (1923), which, apart from the addition of the Dodecanese in 1947, was to draw the final frontier of Greece.

During World War II, Greece fought gallantly against greatly superior Italian forces which invaded from occupied Albania late in 1940. Mussolini's troops had expected to meet little resistance, but all Italian counter-offensives were beaten back in what was virtually a spontaneous uprising by the Greeks. By 1941, however, the German timetable had caught up with Greece and in little more than three months the Greek campaign was over when Crete fell to a spectacular airborne invasion. The Ionian islands were officially annexed by Italy, eastern Macedonia and Thrace by Bulgaria, while the rest of the country was divided into German, Italian and Bulgarian occupation zones. Greece was again dominated by foreign powers and during the occupation period the country experienced extreme hardships. Food shortages became famines, and it was estimated that almost 300,000 people died in the winter of 1941-2. Probably more than defeat and foreign occupation, the horror of hunger, combined with the atrocities committed by the occupation forces, cemented the will of the Greek people and widespread resistance developed. Guerilla warfare aided by allied powers, in particular Britain, succeeded in liberating Athens in October 1944, but the country's reconstruction was made impossible by the civil war against communist factions which lasted until 1949.

Among the resistance movements during the occupation, the one led by the communists (EAM) was undoubtedly the strongest. Initially aided by Britain, this guerilla movement lost British support in 1943 when Britain became concerned with what would happen in Greece when the Axis powers were defeated. Military support shifted to the right-wing, royalist-orientated guerillas (EDES) but ultimately it fell to Britain to attempt to resolve the dispute between these two factions. The bitterness was more than Britain could handle and the evils of German occupation were compounded by the greater evils of an underground civil war. With the end of hostilities in Europe in the spring of 1945, Russia, which hitherto had tacitly approved the British efforts in Greece, now decided to intervene on the side of EAM. The 1944-9 period was, therefore, one of continual bloodshed and terrorism and Greece was, in reality, the battleground for eastern and western ideologies. The British, preoccupied with troubles at home, appealed to the United States in a bid to save Greece from becoming a communist satellite. A us economic mission was dispatched and temporarily given a major role in the EDES government and a military mission aided the reorganisation of the regular Greek army that had come into being. American intervention succeeded in squashing Russian support, and the communist factions began burying their arms and burning their insignia. To strengthen the country's links with the West, Greece was admitted to NATO in 1952. Its friction with Britain over Cyprus ended when the island became independent in 1959-60. In 1962 Greece became the first associated member of the European Economic Community.

In conclusion it should be stressed that Greece has been dominated by foreign interests since she freed herself from Turkish rule in the 1820s. In the years that have elapsed, Greece has always been treated primarily as a vital strategic Mediterranean base at the expense of her national sovereignty. Modern Greek history reflects all of the tragedy of ancient Greek literature and further aspects of its complex politics will be treated in Chapter 3.

POPULATION

The demographic development of Greece has been radically

upset by the political events of this century, in particular by the Greek-Turkish exchanges and by the losses of World War II and the civil war. The 1961 census gave a total population of 8,388,553, of which 43.3 per cent was urban, 12.9 per cent semi-urban and 43.8 per cent rural. The 1951 census had shown a population of 7,632,801, indicating a 9.9 per cent increase between 1951 and 1961 compared with 2.3 per cent for the 1941 to 1951 period which straddled the war years.

Since 1961, however, Greece has been faced with the possibly unique prospect of a population more or less stable or even declining. This is related to low birth rates and high emigration, particularly to other European countries. The effect of emigration on the Greek population is profound, particularly when the drain of the youthful component of the economically active population is considered. The tendency towards a progressively older population and a diminishing labour supply poses problems for the country's economic growth. Infant mortality has been steadily falling during the post-war years, but the low rate of population increase is undoubtedly due to the fact that 85 per cent of the annual emigrants are aged between fifteen and thirty-nine. At the same time the rise in life expectancy from forty, the pre-war average, to sixty-five at the present time, has considerably altered the age structure of the population.

It is often said that Greek emigration is a response to more or less ephemeral psychological impulses, but the high rate of unemployment that has plagued Greece for decades has made it necessary for Greeks to leave their country and seek job opportunities elsewhere. This is also the reason behind the present high rate of internal migration. The rate of population increase (1951-61) in the Greater Athens area and in the country's principal towns and cities substantially exceeded the overall national increase, reflecting the high level of movement from rural to urban areas. Thus the population of Athens increased by 34.4 per cent, Salonica by 27.4 per cent, Larisa by 35.0 per cent and Iraklion by 20.1 per cent. Such a movement is leading to a drastic redistribution of the country's population, the economic implications of which are great.

RELIGION

Greece is now the only officially Orthodox country in the world. Ninety-four per cent of the population are members of the Church, which is virtually a symbol of Greek nationality and an essential part of Hellenism. So closely identified are church and nation that the exchange of Greek and Turkish populations after the first world war was carried out mainly on a religious basis. Although it is not autocratic in the Roman Catholic sense, the church is invested with great authority and prestige and has been deeply involved in the political life of the country. This is perhaps best illustrated by the role played by Archbishop Makarios in the Cyprus issue. Within Greece itself, successful resistance bands were organised and led by priests during the War of Independence and World War II.

The doctrine of the Greek Church is largely that of the Trinitarian western churches, though differences which have developed over the centuries have hindered communion between east and west. During the seventeenth century Orthodoxy was strongly influenced by Calvinism and attempts towards a union between the Orthodox and Protestant churches were common. It is significant that today the Anglican and Orthodox Churches are in communion, whereas a wide doctrinal gulf still separates Roman Catholicism and Orthodoxy.

The Church in Greece recognises the spiritual primacy of the Oecumenical Patriarch of Constantinople, but otherwise it is a self-governing body administered by the Holy Synod under the presidency of the Archbishop of Athens and All Greece. It has no jurisdiction over the Church in Crete, nor over the Church of the Dodecanese, both of which come directly under the Oecumenical Patriarch.

To the western eye the Orthodox Church is full of ritual and mysticism, and in some rural areas this is often interwoven with superstition and even pagan beliefs. Monasticism plays an important part by providing the bishops and other high officers.

Bishops are celibate but the pastoral clergy are allowed to marry. The numerous monasteries offer to travellers hospitality which may be the only accommodation available in some of the remoter areas. A unique monastic community consisting of twenty monasteries and other religious settlements is found on the easternmost peninsula of Chalcidice. This is the self-governing community of Mount Athos from which females are barred. The Greek Government recognised its autonomy in the 1920s and it is administered by a council of four members and an assembly of twenty, one deputy from each monastery. Mount Athos is subject to the spiritual jurisdiction of the Oecumenical Patriarch. Of the twenty ruling monasteries, seventeen are Greek, one Russian, one Serbian and one Bulgarian. *Sketes* or dependent communities are subject to one or other of the ruling monasteries. The monasteries are classed as idiorrhythmic or cenobitic. In the former the monks are allowed to own property, whereas in the latter all possessions are held in common. Hermits and monks who follow a semi-eremitical form of life also feature in Mount Athos.

Although complete religious freedom is recognised in Greece, proselytising from or interference with the Orthodox Church is forbidden. According to the 1961 census, there were, apart from the 8,118,000 adherents to the Orthodox faith, 35,000 Roman and Greek Catholics, 10,200 Armenian Christians, 15,000 Protestants, 8,000 Jehovah's Witnesses, 108,000 Moslems and 5,800 Jews. The latter are found mainly in Salonica and are descendants of Spanish-Jewish refugees of the fourteenth century. The largest Roman Catholic populations are found in the islands and are survivors of Venetian influence.

LANGUAGE

The modern Greek language is spoken by 93 per cent of the inhabitants of the country and also by large numbers around the shores of the eastern Mediterranean. In common with most modern European languages it belongs to the Indo-European family group and provides an unbroken link between ancient Greece and the Greece of today. The modern tongue has preserved a remarkable number of qualities of the original stock and has maintained a unity unparalleled by any other European language. It has been pointed out that the oldest literature of the language, the Homeric poems, is far more intelligible to the modern Greek than Chaucer is to an Englishman.

Ancient Greek knew a number of main dialects, and although they stemmed from a combination of geographical isolation and variation in customs and political organisation they rarely showed any tendency to develop into separate tongues. By the fourth century BC the dialects such as Aeolic, Ionic-Attic, Arcado-Cyprian and Doric were gradually losing their individual significance, and when, following the conquests of Alexander the Great, Greek culture attained a dominating commercial and intellectual significance in the Middle East, a more standardised speech developed as a general instrument of communication. In the first century BC the *Koine* (Common Greek), which rested heavily on the Attic dialect, was the language spoken in Hellenised regions. The Romans made little attempt to displace it, though a number of Latin words and idioms were incorporated into Greek. Written *Koine* continued to be used by the Byzantine

----

The Parthenon is the principal building of the Athenian Acropolis and has shared with the Greeks most phases of their turbulent history. Today it is the country's chief tourist attraction and is a fitting tribute to Greek endurance.

Throughout this century Athens has developed rapidly along Western lines and has spread beyond the formerly isolated hills of the Attic Plain. The view towards Lycabettus Hill indicates the great morphological contrasts between the old town in the foreground and the modern city with its high-rise office and residential blocks.

prose writers until the fifteenth century and it survived the inroads of Islam. It was, however, losing its organic contact with the spoken *Koine* and this gap had reached its widest span by the eighteenth century.

An attempt to bridge the gulf between the written and the popular or demotic language was made by Adamantios Korais (1749-1833). He suggested a compromise between the nearly unintelligible Atticistic Greek and the vernacular by recommending a purified vernacular which would come closer to Attic Greek. An artificial Greek—*Katharevousa*—was thus manufactured and was adopted as the official language after the liberation. Towards the beginning of the nineteenth century a new school arose, consisting at the outset mainly of poets, who upheld the claims of the popular language. The demotic renaissance began in the Ionian Islands and is associated with the names of Solomos and Valaoritis. In 1888 the first important prose work in demotic (John Psycharis's *To Taxidi*) was published, and today it has become the standard spoken and literary language. Nevertheless *Katharevousa* is still used in all official documents, some news reports, scientific treatises and in some university lectures and sermons. The language question is something that has rocked governments throughout this century,

———

Much of the ancient history of Greece is preserved in its archaeological ruins. The Temple of Theseion to the west of the ancient Agora in Athens is a remarkably well preserved Doric structure of the fifth century BC.

On the Saronic island of Aegina the ruins of the Temple of Aphaia overlook the bay of Aghia Marina. The temple was built to celebrate the victory at Salamis (480BC), where the Aegenitans distinguished themselves against Persian forces.

c

especially concerning the roles that demotic and *Katharevousa* should play in education.

Dialects showing variations in pronunciation, construction and vocabulary exist in Greece, but they have been considerably undermined since the introduction of *Katharevousa*. As a result modern Greek has not those marked variations which are found, for example, in France between standard French and the 'patois,' or in Britain between 'Oxford' English and provincial speech.

NATIONAL CHARACTERISTICS

It is always difficult to characterise a nation without resorting to gross over-generalisations. It can be said, however, that the Greeks display most of the characteristics associated with the Mediterranean temperament. They are a volatile, vibrant people with a passion for noise, crowds and conversation. Adjectives particularly apt in describing their personality are generous, curious, sensuous, frank and hospitable. A characteristic they share with other Mediterranean countries is their attitude towards time. The clock is no master of the Greeks and they find it distasteful to organise their activities to external limits. The rapid expansion of Athens and other large centres has meant that city people find the need of hurry and punctuality entering their lives, but away from working hours the old attitude of 'passing' time rather than 'using' it is still widely prevalent.

The Greeks, in a geographical sense, are a European people and have always aped western ideas and attitudes, yet in the past their history has forced them to look towards the Middle East and they share a number of characteristics with the people of this area. Many would argue that the Greeks are a curious mixture of eastern and western, and that the westernisation of their culture is little more than a veneer. It is in the towns and cities that western influence is most marked, but even in Athens the colours of the Orient are strongly represented.

Out of this crisis of identity certain national characteristics have developed which are essentially Greek. Self-esteem is paramount and its essence is inviolability and freedom. It is known as *philotimo,* which is honour rather than pride, and it is basic to a Greek's personal being, his status within a family, village and district, and above all to his nationalism. Individualism and improvisation, two important aspects of the Greek character, rest on *philotimo.* It also underlies his nonchalance, his tendency to take unnecessary risks and his courage, examples of which abound in history. To the democratically-minded Greek, *philotimo* is something which dissolves all class barriers, for everyone, ignorant or educated, wealthy or poor, is equal to everyone else.

Self-esteem and self-dependence in no way undermine family life. In fact the family unit is very much stronger than that of Britain or the United States. The Greek family thinks and acts as an organic whole and it is extremely important that no member bring shame or dishonour to the group. Close ties are constantly kept with the family even when physical separation takes place. Greek emigrants send annually large sums of money for the support of the family or for the education or dowering of a relative. Although dowryless marriages are now becoming more common and the obligation for the eldest son to see all his sisters married before himself is no longer so strict, it is still considered a point of honour in many families. Greek society is patterned on the family unit:

I do not envy others for their vineyards and their gardens,
I envy only those who can stay in one place.
And most I envy those who have brothers and first cousins
To grieve with them and rejoice with them
And to help each other when anything befalls.

(Cretan folk-song)

2

The Regions and the Capital

THE natural environment has led to difficulty in internal communications, and consequently to the development of isolated communities. The many conquerors who ruled Greece from ancient times to the nineteenth century found it extremely difficult, if not impossible, to impose nation-wide political and economic control. Regionalism is still very strong, and even with the country's national road improvements many of the remoter areas are extremely provincial in outlook and isolated from the main developments in national life. This has naturally led to great inequalities in social and economic development, and one of the prime objectives of contemporary governments has been to speed up the process of development in backward areas, while attempting at the same time to preserve the regional character of the countryside and its people.

MACEDONIA AND THRACE

The two most northerly provinces are called 'new provinces' because of their late incorporation into the Kingdom of Greece. They are separated from peninsular Greece by the mountain ranges of Olympus and the Pindus and form part of the Balkan periphery. The large river valleys of the Axios (Vardar), Strymon, Nestos and Evros are geographically the continuation of the river valleys of Serbia and Bulgaria. This has ensured an unsettled history for this northern area and political boundaries have constantly been in a state of flux. Both Macedonia and Thrace are terms for larger geographical areas extending beyond the frontiers of Greece. Greek Thrace is now limited to the area between the rivers Nestos and Evros, and numerous boundary disputes have occurred between the Greek and Turkish sections of this historical area. Similarly the Macedonian question has resulted in a purely artificial frontier between its Greek and Yugoslav sections.

The regions and principal towns of Greece

The north first rose to power in the middle of the fourth century BC with the State of Philip of Macedon. Gradually it became consolidated into a strong political unit that extended into Thessaly, and by 336BC, the year of his assassination, Philip was military commander of the Greek city states of the mainland and archipelago. The Macedonian Empire was inherited by Philip's son, Alexander, who gave Greek culture a more universal appeal which blossomed into the Hellenistic civilisation. With the coming of Rome the whole of northern Greece was placed under the authority of the Roman governor of Macedonia. Salonica became the seat of provincial administration and the great commercial highway, the Via Egnatia, linked it with Durazzo and Byzantium. The close ties with Constantinople brought great prosperity to northern Greece, and by the thirteenth century AD Salonica had become a commercial and intellectual metropolis truly earning the epithet of 'the city of graces.' A long period of stagnation came with Ottoman domination, and Greek Macedonia and Thrace remained in Turkish hands until the early decades of this century.

Northern Greece comprises 32.4 per cent of the total area of Greece and has 26.8 per cent of its population with one-third of the total cultivated area. The presence of large Turkish estates and of extensive malarial lowlands prevented the development of the north until after 1924. Subsequently the region has made great economic progress and in recent years public works such as land reclamation, both drainage and irrigation, and major road improvements have transformed the landscape. Mechanised agriculture has proceeded at a greater rate than in any other part of Greece, and cereals, tobacco and cotton are important export crops. The North of Greece Regional Development Service is particularly active in promoting the economic potential of Macedonia and Thrace. In 1969 a series of studies resulted, for the first time ever, in a detailed analysis of the structure of production in northern Greece and of its possibilities for further expansion.

The era of prosperity is particularly noticeable in the towns and cities, and Salonica, Edessa, Kavalla and Alexandroupolis have been completely modernised to meet the contemporary demands on their functions. Salonica (population 400,000) is the capital of the north and the second city of Greece. It is the natural centre of communications with the country's Balkan neighbours. The city is also the residence of the Minister for Northern Greece and the home of a flourishing university. Developing industries in the interior are having a significant effect on Salonica's harbour, long rendered idle by the competition of Piraeus, and the city itself has been successful in establishing an industrial complex, its nucleus being an oil refinery with subsidiary petrochemical and ammonia plants. Since 1950 an effective development programme has been undertaken, supervised by the Chamber of Commerce and the Port of Salonica Authority. Extensive replanning of the centre has transformed Salonica into a modern city, though the higher part of the town still retains some of the old Turkish atmosphere. The Salonica trade fair is one of the most important commercial events in the Balkans and eastern Mediterranean, a reflection of the position the city merits in international commerce. The 1970 fair featured 800 Greek industrial and handicraft concerns and a total of 2,200 exhibitors from thirty-eight countries. The fair was revived in 1926 and continues the tradition of the commercial fair, held in the Middle Ages as part of the festivities of St Demetrius.

EPIRUS

Throughout the course of history Epirus has been remote and one of the most backward of Greek provinces. This is partly explained by its position and by the relief of the land. The country is mountainous, possessing but one significant plain bordering the Gulf of Amvrakia, and the ranges of limestone, sandstone and schist trend parallel to the coast, forming formidable barriers to communication. The backwardness is also due to its long subjection to Turkish rule, for until 1912 the Graeco-Turkish frontier followed the Arakthos river, which drains to the Amvrakian Gulf. The Epirots rose repeatedly against the Turks in the eighteenth and nineteenth centuries, but, deprived of outside assistance, very little was achieved.

The frontier with Albania is determined by no natural feature and was subject to much dispute before the final demarcation in 1921. It runs across the grain of the country and cuts into two approximately equal parts a natural region that extends from the Amvrakian Gulf to the plains of central Albania. Greece still claims the territory of 'northern' Epirus which was conquered by the Greeks against the Italians during World War II; in fact it has been said that this was Mussolini's most humiliating setback.

Epirus contains a population of around half a million and much of the highlands are covered with denuded forests and grazing grounds for migratory herds led by Kustovlach shepherds. The nomadic Vlachs emerge in the history of medieval Greece, their language being a dialect of Romanian. Today they form an insignificant minority and their language is gradually being replaced by Greek. Cereals, tobacco and vines are important Epirot products, but in general agriculture is inefficient. Ioannina is the capital of the province and the focal point in the communication system. It became famous at the turn of the nineteenth century as the capital of Ali Pasha, whose domain included the whole province, Acarnania, Thessaly and Albania. Prevenza and Arta act as outlets for the agricultural produce of Epirus and the former has improved harbour facilities and sea communications with Corfu and Piraeus.

A study of the development problems of Epirus was started by a group of Greek and European experts in 1957. A development programme for 1960-4 was published and the 'Regional Development Service in Epirus' has been actively organised in the area's recent progress. Road improvements and the opening of the car ferry between Brindisi and Igoumenitsa have had some effect in breaking down the isolation of this lagging region.

THESSALY

The province of Thessaly, liberated from the Turks in 1881, consists of a vast inland plain surrounded on all sides by high mountain ranges—Olympus to the north, the Pindus to the west, Ossa and Pelion to the east and Othris to the south. The plain, which is topographically divided into the upper or Trikkala basin and the lower or Larisa basin, is drained by the river Peneus which reaches the Aegean Sea via the Vale of Tempe.

Thessaly was regarded as a granary in classical times, but the backward farming which prevailed well into this century is related to the prolonged Turkish system of land holding and the general inability of the population to control the plain's water supply. Thessaly had also for centuries been the scene of un-remitting warfare, a factor which hindered development. From the third century AD until the Turkish occupation, Goths, Huns, Bulgars, Serbs and Franks pillaged and burned, and the prov-ince was incorporated into a number of short-lived kingdoms. The Turkish agricultural system, with its large estates and serf labour, prevented any real social and economic advancement.

During this century land reforms, reclamation and flood control works have considerably increased the agricultural pro-ductivity of the province. The farming skill of the refugee element from Asia Minor also helped to raise the standard of output and today the degree of mechanisation is second only to Macedonia. Trikkala (population 28,000) is the chief town of the upper plain and Larisa (55,391) is the capital of the whole province. The port of Volos (49,221) is Thessaly's mari-time outlet and its important sea connections with Piraeus and Salonica, together with its oil-works, tanneries and textile and cigarette factories, make it a commercial centre of some import-ance. Volos has been rapidly rebuilt since 1955, when a series of earthquakes brought destruction to the town and a large number of villages in the surrounding district.

THE IONIAN ISLANDS

The Ionian Islands are strung in a chain off the coast of western Greece. They are sometimes called the *Heptanesus* (Seven Islands) and include Corfu, Leucas, Paxos, Ithaca, Zante,

Cephalonia, Cythera and innumerable small islets. These predominantly limestone islands are mountainous in character, with rocky coasts that cannot be easily approached from the sea. There are a number of alluvial plains and spring-fed areas where cultivation can be maintained throughout the year.

The exposed position of the Ionian Islands at the entry to the Adriatic has involved them in centuries of attack by raiders and in many political changes. They have long served as ports of call between Greece and the western Mediterranean and have passed into Byzantine, Norman, Venetian, Neapolitan, French, Russian, British and Italian hands. Alone among the Greek lands, however, the Ionian Islands escaped Turkish domination. They were ceded by Britain to Greece in 1864.

The successive foreign occupiers built roads and hospitals, reformed education, law and agriculture, and in general provided material and spiritual advantages denied to Ottoman Greece. The Venetians have left the most lasting cultural traces, particularly in religion and in church and town architecture. Much of the fine Venetian architecture of Zante was destroyed in a devastating earthquake in the summer of 1953. During World War II the Ionian Islands again reverted to Italy for a brief period, when an Italian governor was appointed and Italian currency and postage stamps were introduced. Following the Anglo-Italian armistice in September 1943, Italy failed to defend the islands against German landings.

Corfu is the most densely populated and commercially important island. It is served by most ships on the Adriatic-Piraeus line as well as by boats which ply daily to Piraeus. The island is intensively cultivated where conditions permit, and one-third of the farmed acreage is devoted to vineyards. Cereals, olives, vegetables and citrus fruits are also important. The island capital, in spite of severe bombing in 1943, has preserved much of its historical character and is the official summer residence of the Greek royal family.

CRETE

Crete, the largest of all Greek islands and the fourth in size in the Mediterranean, was the centre of Europe's earliest civilisation. Its geographical position at the junction of three continents has made it a natural stepping-stone whereby cultural influences from Africa and Asia penetrated Europe. The size and isolation of the island has encouraged independence, but during historical times this was achieved for a short time only after 1898, when, supported by Britain, the Turks were compelled to recognise the autonomy of Crete. Union with Greece was finally proclaimed in 1913.

The relief of Crete consists of a rugged mountainous backbone extending the full length of the island and reaching well over 6,000ft in Mounts Ida, Leuka and Dhikti. Lower-lying isthmuses separate the massif into four mountain blocks. The largest area of lowland is the plain of Mesara in the south, but small strips of coastal plain are found in the north. Along most of the south coast the mountains fall steeply to the sea and there are few adequate harbours. The island is composed mainly of limestone and no river worthy of the name exists.

Unlike the Ionian Islands, the Venetian occupation of Crete was oppressive and the island was economically exploited to a degree that made it the most valuable possession of Venice. The Cretan peasantry, however, were for the most part broken-spirited serfs whose labours went entirely to the enrichment of their lords. The character of the foreign rule was relaxed only when it became apparent that the Turks were bent upon the conquest of the island. Remarkable fortifications were carried out which still survive in such towns as Iraklion, Canea, Rethimnon and Sitia. Crete finally fell into Turkish hands and from 1670 onwards the brutal tyranny provoked numerous popular revolts.

The resistance of Candia (Iraklion) to the Turkish onslaught was legendary, the siege lasting twenty-three years. The last

Turks left Crete at the time of the transfer of population in 1923, but Turkish influence is still strongly felt, especially in the towns with their bazaars and ruined mosques.

The positional significance of the island was again revealed during World War II when it fell into German hands in 1941. After undaunted resistance it was liberated in 1944, since when its economic recovery has made great progress. In particular there has been a revolution in the field of tourism, and large modern hotels are a characteristic feature of Iraklion and other towns. Daily boat services link the northern towns with Piraeus, and Canea (population 38,000), the provincial capital, and Iraklion (64,000) the island's chief commercial centre and port, are served by regular daily flights to Athens.

THE AEGEAN ISLANDS

The islands of Greece are numbered in their hundreds and the majority of them have played a colourful part in classical mythology and history. For administrative purposes they are divided into a number of groups and some are attached to the mainland for local government purposes. The Argo-Saronic islands of Aegina, Poros, Hydra and Septses belong to Attica, the Northern Sporades group of Skiathos, Skopelos and Skyros are closely associated with Thessaly, and the northern islands of Thasos and Samothrace are linked with Kavalla and Alexandroupolis respectively.

The Cyclades or Central Islands form one of the most important groups. In classical times they were regarded as forming a circle around the island of Delos, the traditional birthplace of Apollo. Delos gave rise to an important religious cult which led to the development of a great commercial city, now an archaeologist's paradise. The contemporary pivot of the Cyclades is Syra, which contains the town of Ermoupolis, the hub of shipping routes in the central Aegean. Ermoupolis has a large Roman Catholic quarter which stems from the Venetian Duchy of Naxos in the Middle Ages.

For the most part the Cycladic Islands are rock-bound and barren in appearance, and lowlands and coastal plains are few. Their physical characteristics vary from the weird volcanic landscapes of Santorini (Thera), racked with earthquake scars, to the more hospitable low-lying features of Syra. In general the way of life is primitive, but tourism has opened up a number of islands such as Myconos, and standards of living have been raised considerably.

The Dodecanese, sometimes referred to as the Southern Sporades, consists of twelve main islands lying off the coast of Asia Minor. Rhodes is the largest, and from 1309 to 1522 it was the Mediterranean headquarters of the Knights of St John. The extensive fortifications on the island, and on Kos, still bear witness to the continual struggle between Christian and Islamic forces. The Dodecanese were occupied by the Turks until 1912 and by the Italians until 1945. The islands were officially recognised as part of Greece on 31 January 1948.

THE PELOPONNESUS

The Corinth Canal, completed in 1893, separates the Peloponnesus from the Greek mainland. The idea of piercing the four-mile-long isthmus dates back to ancient times and it was Nero who actually started operations in AD67, though the work was not completed. The canal shortens the distance from Piraeus to Brindisi by 200 miles and it is capable of accommodating comparatively large vessels, although a current of 1-3 knots necessitates a cautious passage.

The Peloponnesus forms the southern extremity of the Balkan peninsula and takes its name from the ancient island of Pelops. In the Middle Ages it was known as the Morea, due to the fact that the mulberry flourished in the country. It is a highland region with more than half of its area above 1,500ft. An irregular series of limestone mountains, encircling Arcadia, forms the backbone of the country from which mountainous promontories reach the sea in all directions. In the north and west the uplands are fringed by an almost continuous coastal belt of varying width but extending for some two hundred miles, and unique in Greece. In the south and east the three basin plains of Messinia, Laconia and Argolis open to deep gulfs and form compact, isolated units.

The imposing ruins of the Peloponnesus illustrate more fully and comprehensively four thousand years of history than anywhere else in Europe. Mycenaean, Greek, Roman, Byzantine, Frankish, Venetian and Turkish remains reveal the province's complex evolution. In 1821 it was Germanos, the Bishop of Patras, who raised the standard of revolt against the Turks, and the Peloponnesus formed the core of the early nineteenth-century kingdom. Nauplion, in the Argolis district, was the first capital of independent Greece. Otho, first king of Greece, disembarked at Nauplion in 1833, remaining until the government was removed to Athens in 1834.

A consequence of the physical geography of the Peloponnesus is that settlement and economic activity tend to be peripheral. Tripolis (population 18,500) is the only important inland centre situated at the crossroads of the peninsula. The majority of Peloponnesian cities which had a great past survive today as small and local market centres. Sparta (10,412), the ancient warlike and puritanical rival of Athens, keeps only the reputation of its glory. Corinth, which stands on the isthmus, has benefited little from its maritime canal, but continues to export the famous sun-dried currants. The major town is Patras (100,000), the third city of Greece and the third port after Piraeus and Salonica. It is a busy commercial and manufacturing town and exports the produce of the fertile northern coastlands, particularly Corinthian currants. Patras has direct sailings to a number of foreign seaports and is one of the terminals of the regular car ferries from Italy. Kalamata (38,210) is the main southern town and is an important manufacturing centre. It has regular air, train and coach services to Athens.

STEREA HELLAS

Central Greece is officially called Sterea Hellas and extends from the Sperkhios valley in the north, southwards to the Gulf of Corinth. Locally the region is known as the Roumeli and the inhabitants proudly insist on their Roman heritage. In the west the geographical features of Epirus are found in the Aetolia and Acarnania areas, though the land is lower in altitude and agriculturally more productive. The Ambracian and Agrinion plains are richly farmed areas with a high acreage under tobacco. The eastern part of the province is broken up into a number of geographical and historical entities whose names today, Locris, Phocis, Doris, Boeotia and Attica, are descendants of the classical city states. Situated off the eastern coast of Sterea Hellas is the large island of Euboea, exhibiting both insular and continental characteristics. Its chief town is Chalkis (population 25,000), whose prosperity is related to industrial development and a rich agricultural hinterland.

The Boeotian district was already famous in classical times for its rich resources. Cereals, horses and cattle went side by side with a wealth of marble and iron ore. Today much of its agricultural importance is based on the reclaimed Lake Copais which brought 5,000 acres of land into cultivation. The draining of the lake, first undertaken by the engineers of Alexander the Great, was finally accomplished at the turn of the century by an Anglo-French company. The central artery of Boeotia is the main road and railway that link Athens with northern Greece, and along which the main market towns of Thebes and Livadia are situated. To the north, in the Sperkhios valley, the town of Lamia (population 26,000) has important marketing and industrial functions.

The mountainous peninsula of Attica forms the south-western extremity of Sterea Hellas, and its history is largely the history of Athens. The plain of Attica itself is a dry and infertile area sloping gently to the coast of the Saronic Gulf. It is drained intermittently by the river Kifissos and its tributaries, and is surrounded by an amphitheatre of high mountain ranges. The presence of several outliers of lower hills in the centre of the plain determined the site of ancient Athens which developed around the Acropolis Hill (512ft) at a distance of three miles from the Saronic Gulf. Other site advantages were the presence of roadsteads at Phaleron and Piraeus and ultimately these were connected to the ancient city by the Long Walls. After centuries of decline and stagnation Athens is again a flourishing city and forms the centre of a large metropolitan region covering one hundred square miles of the Attic plain. Athens is concerned mainly with the administrative and service functions, while Piraeus is not only Greece's principal port, but also constitutes its main industrial concentration.

THE CAPITAL

At the conclusion of the Greek War of Independence Athens was little more than a provincial market town with a few thousand inhabitants. The settlement was concentrated on the northern and eastern slopes of the Acropolis Hill and caused

The Orthodox church continues the traditions of the Byzantine empire into modern Greece and colourful pomp and ritual accompany services. At the Monastery of Iviron in Mount Athos an important feast is celebrated on 15 August and is attended by many church dignitaries and theologians.

The Athos monasteries are renowned for their art treasures, many derived from rich endowments and earlier possessions in Asia Minor, Russia and the Balkans. Vatopedi houses important medieval icons and a fine manuscript library.

many a nineteenth-century writer to comment cynically that the least ruined objects were the ancient ruins themselves. By 1842 some redevelopment had taken place but the new residences were regarded as 'pearls in a dunghill, scattered at wide intervals among the cottages and ruins.'

The reconstruction and expansion of the city stemmed from its acceptance as the capital of the newly liberated nation. Other centres, such as Corinth, Patras and Nauplion, were considered, but the historic claim of Athens outweighed the advantages that some of these cities could offer. In 1833 the seat of government was transferred to Athens from the Peloponnesian town of Nauplion which had acted as the provisional capital and headquarters of the National Army.

During the nineteenth century Athens grew from a village of rubble to the political, commercial and cultural centre of Greece, and its boundaries were eventually merged with those of the expanding port of Piraeus. Yet the early city was an apology for a capital. It had no adequate water supply, few made-up roads, and was said to suffer from dust and politics. In an attempt to develop the character of the city in a manner befitting its new status, the government had early appointed foreign and Greek architects to plan its expansion. After considerable local

———

In spite of great drives towards modernisation, traditional methods of cultivation persist, especially in the islands where smallholdings and primitive technology exist in an agriculturally restrictive environment.

The Aluminium de Grèce, situated at Antikyra Bay on the Gulf of Corinth, is the largest metallurgical plant in Greece. Its adjacent model housing estates were inspired by the architecture of the Greek island communities.

D

CHIEF GOVERNMENT COMMERCIAL AND
EDUCATIONAL ESTABLISHMENTS

* UNDERGROUND STATIONS

~ BOUNDARY OF TURKISH TOWN

0   ¼ mile

Street pattern of central Athens. The nineteenth-century town covered a small area. It was located to the north of the Acropolis and extended from Hadrian's Arch (A) in the east to the ancient Diplyon Gate in the west (C), and northwards to the church of St Theodore (B). The principal feature of the new town is a triangle, the base of which, Hermes Street (E) cuts through the old quarter. The remaining sides are Piraeus (G) and Stadium (F) streets. Two large squares, Omonoia (D) and Syntagma (Constitution) (M), occupy the apexes of the triangle, but there is no corresponding development in the west where the ancient cemetery (N) is located. The triangle is bisected by Athinas Street (H) and parallel to it is Eolou Street (I) which is continued as the great north road Patission (L). Other major thoroughfares are Venizelou (J) and Academias (K) streets which lie parallel with Stadium. As a result of this triangular arrangement the modern city has expanded in a series of regular grid-iron blocks whose orientations are governed by the central complex.

reaction to various proposals the new Athens emerged in a geometric street form centred on Omonia Square, three-quarters of a mile to the north of the Acropolis and the old settlement. Today this chequer-board pattern of streets with large squares and boulevards stands in marked contrast to the haphazard arrangement of narrow lanes in the old town. By 1840 plans for Piraeus had been approved and the town was developed on principles reminiscent of its classical predecessor.

Initially the population of Athens had not expanded as much as had been expected. The census of 1853 records a figure of 30,590 and at the close of Otho's reign in 1861 it had risen to 41,298. The annexation to Greece of new territories greatly increased the growth of the capital area after 1860. A complementary development was the opening of the Athens-Piraeus railway in 1869 which encouraged development along the route, particularly at New Phaleron. The Attica railway, established around 1885, also led to expansion towards the north at Halandri, Maroussi, Kifissia and Patissia. Towards the end of the century the population of Athens was around 180,000 and the urban linkage zone with Piraeus was more strongly developed.

The expansion throughout this century has been typical of the situation in many capitals of emerging small nations where the greatest percentage of cultural, business and administrative functions are concentrated in one city which has developed under the pressures of composite factors of geography and economics. In part, however, the demographic growth of Athens since 1900 is also related to political incidents outside the control of Greece. Under the Greek-Turkish population exchanges the Athens area was forced to accept around 300,000 refugees for whom shelter and employment had to be provided. Others flooded in during the Civil War. Migration to Athens has continued, and in the 1950-61 period the capital absorbed over 300,000 people from provincial areas.

The population of the metropolitan area, which includes Piraeus and a number of contiguous townships, has now reached the 2 million mark (1,850,000 in 1961), which is roughly equivalent to one-quarter of the total population of Greece, and to more than half the urban population of the country. The regional planning problems stemming from this are great, and modern Athens, like all large cities, suffers from its own problems of overcrowding, atmospheric pollution and acute traffic congestion. Solving the problems of Athens depends not only on a proper master plan for the city itself, but much more on the successful application of the principles of regional planning. The reorganisation of the built-up area is under discussion and a decentralisation policy which will benefit the country as a whole is slowly being implemented. Valuable work is being undertaken by the Athens Centre of Ekistics (Settlement) in its Capital of Greece Project. This explores the growth structure, as well as alternative future development possibilities for Athens, and part of the research concerns a comparison of Athens with cities of similar population size. Already there have been proposals for the creation of satellite towns outside the Athens basin, but within a radius of 30 miles of the city centre. It is claimed that these growth towns would directly aid a decentralisation policy. The problem is acute, for Athens is the country's great pole of attraction and keeps growing, largely at the expense of provincial districts.

3

How the Country is Run

THE Greeks have been described as the most politically obsessed people on earth, with the result that political life is both intensely active and highly unstable. The periods of democracy, dictatorship, republic, oligarchy, tyranny and 'crown democracy,' the number and variety of political parties, and the short average life of governments, reveal the political involvement of the Greeks, which almost amounts to a national pastime. Between the country's liberation in 1944 and the military *coup d'état* in 1967, forty-one governments held office in a period of twenty-three years. Sometimes there were five or six governments within the span of a single year, and this obviously has precluded any continuity in economic and social progress.

The instability of Greece's politics has often been related to the volatile, hot-headed and highly individualistic temperament of her people. It has been said that the political factions fight each other with the fierce ardour of the wars of the ancient city states. Yet the internal strife is also a reflection of the country's precarious external politics in relationship to its strategic importance in south-east Europe. Since regaining independence in the nineteenth century, its sovereignty has been subject to the veto of whatever greater power looms over the eastern Mediterranean, whether it be Britain, Germany or the United States. Greece now occupies a position in an otherwise communist-run Balkans, and early fell victim to the so-called 'cold war.' It was natural that Greece should be attracted by the security system of NATO and by 1952 the country was receiving considerable American

57

military and economic aid. In 1968, as a result of events in Czechoslovakia and Russian threats against Yugoslavia and Albania, ties with NATO were strengthened and a joint naval force was established in the eastern Mediterranean with Greece supplying the ships when needed. The attachment of Greece to the EEC is yet another bid for economic and moral support from the western world and, in reality, is a recognition of the country's vulnerability in world affairs.

The revolution of 21 April 1967 revealed to the world at large both the internal and external political weaknesses of the country. Initially it was reported to have stemmed from the clash between the right-wing monarchists and militia and the communist-biased leftists who threatened to undermine constitutional monarchy. But the junta's claim that it had moved to thwart a communist takeover was soon recognised to be a minor factor in the *coup*. In the thirty-two years since the Metaxas dictatorship Greek politics had been firmly in the hands of the Palace and its right-wing supporters. Despite the volatility of Greek politics this control never wavered and had never been seriously challenged. The exception came under Papandreou when a 'new' politics emerged in Greece which threatened the old game of superficial politics. In 1964-5 an air of political freedom entered Greek politics and challenged the traditional distribution of power. There is strong support for the view that the *coup* took place in order to prevent the victory of the Centre Union party at the polls.

This is not to say, however, that fear of communism was unimportant. In Greece communism is not an abstract threat but a living memory of something that tore the country apart just over twenty years ago. The final defeat of the communist forces by the National Army in 1949 left the country in a devastated condition. According to official figures, the civil war cost 40,000 lives, but unofficial estimates range up to 158,000. Hundreds of thousand of people were made homeless, and the material damage reduced the country to a state not much better than in 1944, following the liberation. Another 80,000 to 100,000 people crossed the border as refugees and were absorbed in the various communist countries, the largest colony being at Tashkent in Central Asia. These memories are an ever-present background to Greek politics today.

Largely in view of the political developments in Greece since 1944, many have regarded the 1967 revolution as a historical necessity. It is not the purpose of this chapter, however, to take sides in this highly controversial issue. Yet it must be stressed that during the last twenty years Greece has been suffering from an incurable political disease which has been eating away at the national organism. In such an atmosphere of mistrust, dictatorship can be imposed by the Army as an alternative to communism or instability, and even as a guarantee of firm government. Greece desperately needs political stability and there are many people, both inside and outside the country, who have advocated that an authoritarian régime may provide the country with a stable framework in which to grow efficiently. The point, of course, is debatable. History has shown, more often than not, that shared power has been more effective in the long run than absolute power, and that people who take part in the formulation of decisions that have some bearing on their lives tend to be more contented in their work and to achieve better results. Even so, there is no denying the fact that Greece since 1967 has achieved remarkable results in both economic and social reform.

CONSTITUTIONAL MONARCHY WITH A DIFFERENCE

The 1967 *coup* was executed by a military triumvirate of relatively junior officers—Brigadier Stylianos Patakos, Colonel George Papadopoulos and Colonel Nicholas Makarezos. General Gregorios Spandidakis was brought in at the final stages of preparation, with Constantine Kollias, the chief prosecutor of the Supreme Court, providing the civilian façade. The junta, lacking any popular base of support, started to consolidate its position in a series of edicts and the army was quick to issue its orders to the civilian population. The supposed innocence of King

Constantine is now heavily discounted, but an abortive attempt was made by him to overthrow the régime, which culminated in his exile. Papadopoulos continued as Prime Minister and a plebiscite and quick return to democratic rule was promised.

Greece, therefore, is a 'constitutional monarchy' with an exiled king, or to quote Article 2 of the 1968 Constitution, 'the form of Government in Greece is that of a Crowned Democracy.' At present the executive power is exercised by the junta and the cabinet is appointed by them. This is by no means the first time that officers of the Greek army have taken matters into their own hands, nor is it the first time that a reigning monarch has fled the country.

Constitutional monarchy was instituted in Greece in 1843, when, under pressure of a bloodless revolt by the Greek army, King Otho, the first sovereign of the independent State, was compelled to grant a constitution. In honour of his decision the area outside the royal palace (now parliament) was renamed Constitution Square. The appointment of Otho, a Bavarian prince, as the country's first monarch was the decision of a conference held by Greece's European allies in which Britain played an active role. Unfortunately, the undisguised despotism of the Bavarian administration was only slightly modified by the constitution of 1843 and the real needs and aspirations of the Greeks were hardly considered.

Otho was dethroned in 1862 and, largely as the result of British influence again, his place on the throne was taken by Prince George Glucksburg of Denmark. The title of George I as 'King of the Hellenes' (not 'King of Hellas') indicated that he must be a constitutional or even democratic ruler. It is a tribute to his tact that he was able for nearly fifty years to keep his footing in the system set up by the first democratic constitution of 1864. His long and important reign ended in tragic circumstances with his assassination in 1913 by a Greek in the newly occupied city of Salonica.

A leading figure was to emerge during the later part of George I's reign, the Cretan leader Eleutherios Venizelos.

Venizelos, who had distinguished himself during the wars of independence of his home island, became Prime Minister in 1910, when a stormy period of triumphs and disasters began. The construction of a modern democracy on the West European model was his dream and the constitution of 1864 was fully revised with individual liberties guaranteed. Under its revision some of the formal prerogatives of the monarchy were curtailed, but the real powers of the king remained ambiguous. During World War I, the pro-German sympathies of King Constantine, son of George I, led Venizelos to set up a separate national government at Salonica, and in 1917 the king was forced to abdicate in favour of his son Alexander. The accidental death of Alexander in 1920 posed a problem of succession, and in spite of Venizelos' efforts for the younger brother Paul to take the throne, Constantine was recalled and led the campaign against the Turks in Asia Minor. The humiliating defeat leading to the Treaty of Lausanne and the exchange of Greek and Turkish populations again forced Constantine into exile (1922), where he died a few months later.

The abdication was followed by an issue between the republicans and royalists, and in the face of strong military and naval support for a republic, George II, Constantine's successor, left Greece without formally abdicating. A republic was proclaimed on 25 March 1924, but between that date and 1928 Greece suffered ten prime ministers, three general elections, and eleven military *coups*. Venizelos failed to establish anything like moderation in Greek politics during this period and he was destined to die in exile in Paris (1936).

In 1935 a rigged plebiscite voted for the restoration of the monarchy and the return of George II, but a new political rot —Fascism—was spreading across Europe and Greece as well. General John Metaxas seized control of Athens in 1936 and began remodelling the nation along Axis lines. Metaxas operated a police state with concentration camps, torture, the abolition of civil liberties and the rigid censorship of the press. Yet Metaxas built roads, instituted the eight-hour day, the minimum wage and workers' health insurance. Most important, he modernised the Greek army and it was this army which soundly and astonishingly drubbed Mussolini's force in 1940. Metaxas died the following year when Greece became an Axis province.

During the occupation George II again went into exile, this time with his government, which was completely cut off from the country. The lack of all communications led by degrees to the existence of two Greeces, completely different in aspirations, aims and structure. The resistance movement in Greece produced a clash of ideologies between those who were in sympathy with the extreme left, and those who favoured less radical ideas represented by the exiled government. Civil war until 1949 prolonged the misery and insecurity suffered during the occupation. Field-Marshal Papagos, who was mainly responsible for the final victories over the communists, became Prime Minister from 1952 to 1955, and under him and his successor Constantine Karamanlis, a decade of political stability was secured for Greece. 1947 had seen the death of George II and the accession of his brother Paul to the throne.

With four terms in office, Karamanlis reigned as Prime Minister until June 1963, the longest uninterrupted government in Greek history. As a leader he showed surprising magnetism at the polls and velvet-glove firmness in office. Personal grievances between him and the royal family form part of the reason behind his resignation and his exile in Paris since 1963. Karamanlis was succeeded by George Papandreou, but the relative economic and political stability achieved under Karamanlis's government gave way to a period marked by ten governmental changes in the four years up to 1967. This period also witnessed the death of King Paul in March 1964 and the accession of his son Constantine II. The series of short-lived cabinets was followed by a non-political administration which held office from December 1966 charged with the organisation of a general election in May 1967. This was forestalled by the bloodless *coup d'état* of April 1967.

THE CONSTITUTION

This brief and sketchy political history of independent Greece demonstrates that the Greeks delight in constitution-making, a characteristic they share with their ancient forbears. Since the granting of the first constitution in 1843 there have been a number of new or revised constitutions (1864, 1911, 1926 and 1935), the last of which was suspended under the Metaxas dictatorship and restored in 1944. This, however, was replaced after the civil war by a new constitution, preaching liberty of conscience, which came into force on 1 January 1952. Major defects in the 1952 constitution were soon recognised and proposals for its complete revision were widely accepted. The major aims of Karamanlis were to improve the functioning of parliament, strengthen the executive, and protect the nation's free institutions from extremists, in particular to guard against *coups d'état* from all quarters. It was, therefore, somewhat ironical that the revolutionary government of 1967 also laid great importance on a revision of the constitution 'to iron out the misinterpretatons of its provisions.' With parliament suspended, promises were made to put the 'new' constitution to the country in a referendum. After much revision it was voted upon on 29 September 1968, and the result was a large majority in favour of its provisions.

In keeping with earlier constitutions the executive power rests with the king and the ministers appointed (and dismissed) by him. The legislative power is exercised by the king and parliament and the judicial power, in the name of the king, is exercised by the courts. The king is regarded as the supreme lord of the State and the symbol of the nation's unity. Following a general election the king is obliged to appoint as prime minister the leader of the political party with a complete majority in parliament. If no party gains a complete majority, then machinery involving the king, parliament, and the Council of the Nation is introduced in choosing a premier.

One of the aims of the present constitution was to 'clarify some aspects of the King's prerogatives' which had caused controversy in the past. Although the status of the king's family has been reduced in importance, in that only the king and crown prince are entitled to any allowance from the Treasury, the powers of the king, on balance, have been consolidated, and in some instances increased. Following, however, Constantine's self-exile on 13 December 1967, the revolutionary government appointed General Zoitakis as Regent to carry on the duties of the king 'until such time as the Government invites the King to return to Greece.'

The government is composed of the ministerial council under the chairmanship of the prime minister, and up to two vice-premiers, with or without portfolio, may be appointed. The constitution limits the number of ministers to twenty and specifies precisely their competences and areas of responsibility. All ministerial committees and councils are presided over by the prime minister. Under Article 88, no member of parliament, with the exception of the prime minister and the deputy prime ministers, may be appointed a member of the government, even though that person should resign his parliamentary office.

Although the 1967 revolution abolished parliamentary government for what has been termed a 'transitional' period, the constitution introduced a number of innovations aimed at ensuring a more efficient operation of parliament's jurisdictions. Parliament is composed of deputies, elected in accordance with the law through direct, universal and secret ballot by all citizens who have attained the age of twenty-one and have the right to vote. The number of deputies for each electoral district is designated in proportion to the legal population, as determined in the most recent census. Under the new constitution the number of deputies has been reduced by half to a maximum of 150. They must be of Greek citizenship by birth, over twenty-five years of age and in possession of a high-school education diploma or the equivalent. The constitution forbids the election of a deputy for more than three consecutive parliamentary periods. This ruling, however, does not apply to premiers or party leaders.

Not only does parliament at the present time remain shuttered, but certain parts of the constitution are also suspended—particularly those referring to the freedom concept dear to the heart of the Greek. Under Article 14 censorship and the seizure of printed matter is prohibited, except where insults are directed against the church and monarchy or where the disclosure concerns State information or is of an indecent nature. In practice, however, the press has been heavily censored and a number of influential newspapers have been shut down. In February 1968 a first step towards ending censorship was announced, though self-censorship still operates and publishers and editors are liable to prosecution for contents infringing martial law. The freedom of the individual was also abused in the large-scale arrests that accompanied the military junta's rise to power. The question of Greece's political prisoners has led to extensive anti-government campaigns emanating from the western world, with the result that the situation in reality has often been clouded with emotional propaganda. It is known, however, that following the 1967 revolution the police carried out arrests to the tune of 6,000 persons, though the majority were subsequently released. In the latter part of 1968 house detention was lifted and one of the two main islands used as detention centres was closed. In April 1970 the release of over 300 political prisoners, including the composer Theodorakis, indicated a relaxation in the country's detention methods.

POLITICAL PARTIES

It is important to understand that Greece is a land where politics is the preoccupation of practically everyone. As one author recently put it, politics, not Euripides, is the national drama and one which entails the frequent changing of cast and also the play. This point has already been stressed in earlier pages and it is again reflected in the great variety of political parties that appear, disappear and reappear in constant succession. Unlike Britain and the United States, where political parties are highly organised, semi-permanent groups with an elected head, in Greece they tend to be formed by and to reflect the opinions of their leaders. When a leader falls out of favour, as frequently happens, the party, too, disintegrates or reforms under a new title or political doctrine.

With the exception of the extreme communist left, political parties have traditionally lacked any hard-and-fast ideological base. In this ideological vacuum they tend to revolve around a few dominant personalities who are quick to switch their allegiances as they see fit. Party structure and party discipline are concepts alien to Greek politics and new alignments and coalitions are frequent occurrences.

The recent history of Greek political parties, up to the 1967 revolution, revolves around the fortunes of the Centre Union and its struggle for power involving the varying support of other factions. The Centre Union was formed shortly before the 1961 elections by a coalition of the following groups and parties of the Centre : the Liberal Democratic Party led by Papandreou; the Liberal Party (S. Venizelos); the Democratic Union (Tsirimokos); and other splinter groups. The 1961 elections brought Papandreou to its leadership and the party won 34 per cent of the votes cast. The elections returned Karamanlis and the National Radical Union (ERE) with a comfortable majority of 176 seats out of 300. The right-wing ERE had been formed by Karamanlis in 1956 and was the governing party from that date until 1963.

The Centre Union charged that the elections were fixed, and as dissatisfaction with the government grew, pressure built up for new elections which were set for 3 November 1963. The Centre Union emerged as the major party with 42 per cent of the total vote and 47 per cent of the parliamentary seats, 140 out of 300. It was 11 seats short of a parliamentary majority and the Progressive Party (KP) of Markezinis, which won only 2 seats, was unable to provide the necessary support. The remaining 158 were split unequally with 128 for ERE and 30 for the United Democratic Left (EDA). The balance of power, therefore, lay with the left.

The EDA, the extreme left-wing party, was founded in 1951 as a front of the Communist Party, outlawed in 1947. In spite of offers by the EDA of parliamentary support, Papandreou considered co-operation with EDA out of the question, he himself being a rabid anti-communist. New elections were called for and they were scheduled for 16 February 1964. They returned for the first time in over thirty-five years a liberal Centre party and the right found itself in the position of being decidedly the minority party. The election returns and the distribution of seats were as follows:

	Per cent of total vote	*Number of Deputies*	*Per cent of total*
National Radical Union (ERE, Kanellopoulos) and Progressive Party (KP, Markezinis)	35	107	36
Centre Union (EK, Papandreou)	53	171	57
United Democratic Left (EDA, Passalidis)	12	22	7

In spite of the triumph of Papandreou, the palace, the extreme right and the army were still in complete control of the bureaucracy and the security forces and the victory of the Centre Union was not seen as a direct threat. Papandreou undertook the difficult task of balancing the right against the left and pressured for economic and political reform. But his attempts at extensive liberalisation began yet another stormy period in Greek political life. By 1965-6 the sense of security built up under Karamanlis disintegrated into political turmoil with episodes of demonstration and mob violence. The series of events leading to Papandreou's downfall are too complex to discuss here, but they led to his ousting in July 1965, an event which many have regarded as being the most tragic in post-war Greek politics.

In mid-September a new government emerged under the premiership of Stephanopoulos, formerly Papandreou's deputy prime minister. This splinter group, which became known as the Liberal Democratic Centre, survived for eighteen months until December 1966 when Kanellopoulos and the ERE withdrew its support. A caretaker government was then instituted until the elections which were to have taken place on 28 May 1967.

The Greek electoral system is as complex and changeable as the political parties it endeavours to put into office. In the past it has been common for the electoral system to be manipulated in the government's interest and illegal entries in the electoral lists enabling double or multiple voting have been exposed on a large scale. Besides fraud, elections have been marked by violence and threats during campaigns, especially in rural areas. These actions have been levelled against the 1961 elections which again returned the National Radical Union to power and the results were bitterly challenged by opposition forces. Papandreou had attempted to break the control of the rural gendarmerie over the countryside, a measure which was not well received by right wing supporters.

By 1961 the electoral system had become extremely complicated: while retaining the majority system in the provinces, based on the antiquated 1940 census, proportional representation was the method used in the urban centres. It has been shown that refusal to readjust the electoral lists according to the most recent population census resulted in grave disproportions of representation between the urban centres where the centre and left were stronger, and the agrarian regions where the right was powerful. Since 1961 a number of laws have been passed establishing proportional representation as the electoral system and further amendments have been introduced by the present government.

On 29 May 1952 women over twenty-one were given the vote and women over twenty-five were allowed to stand for parliament.

LEGAL SYSTEM

According to the constitution justice is the third authority in the land (after the executive and the legislature) and is the foundation of social peace. Under the Turks the Greeks, in addition to their ecclesiastical institutions and a certain amount of local self-government, retained their judicial independence. As soon as the modern State came into being new courts of law were set up, and from 1835 to the present day they have constituted a complete judicial authority. There have been periods, however, when the judicial system was completely disrupted, particularly during the enemy occupation of World War II when most judges and magistrates resigned or were dismissed. Furthermore, during the periods of various military governments, justice and the rights of the individual have been forced to take a subordinate role in Greek life, a point levelled against the present régime, where according to many 'the laws sleep.' In theory the judiciary is invested with constitutionally protected guarantees securing the independence and impartiality of judicial authority.

The Supreme Court is the court of the State, having also appellate powers. It sits in Athens and is still known by its ancient name of Areopagos. Its duty is to preserve the unity of the legal system and to quash all judgements contrary to the law of the land. It is divided into four sections, three civil and one penal. Below the Supreme Court are the eleven Courts of Appeal with jurisdiction in cases of civil and penal law of second degree, and in exceptional cases of first degree. The courts of first instance, which number fifty-eight, are mixed courts and deal with the more serious offences against the civil and commercial code. They also function as penal courts, and in the towns where courts of first instance sit there are, in addition, criminal courts and juvenile courts. The lowest criminal court is the police court, which has as a rule only one magistrate. The lowest civil court is administered by a Justice of the Peace

E

and it decides civil and commercial cases where no large sums are involved. Greece has 48 police courts and 360 courts of Justices of the Peace.

LOCAL GOVERNMENT

The institution of local self-government has since remote antiquity had its roots deep in the traditions of the Greek people. It is a development of the prevailing independence of the city states of ancient Greece. The Greek willingly accepts the responsibility for local administration, and even under Turkish domination much of this remained in Greek hands. The *dhiamerisma* is the largest administrative unit, but with the exception of the later-acquired northern areas, it tends to be of theoretical rather than of practical importance. Thus the broad divisions of Macedonia, Thrace, Epirus, Thessaly, Sterea Hellas, Peloponnesus, Crete and the island groups, as discussed in Chapter 2, correspond to the broad geographical and historical regions of the country.

Greece is divided into fifty-two *nomes* which are the basic units of administrative decentralisation. To this number should be added Mount Athos, which is an autonomous unit under Greek government. The *nomarch* is generally a competent and well-trained administrator appointed by the Minister of the Interior. He represents the central government in local areas and wields considerable power. His duties include the maintenance of public order and security, the supervision of prisons and hospitals, and the upkeep of roads, railways, bridges and public buildings. Furthermore, he enforces education acts, collects rates and taxes and administers government funds. In office he is superior to all other authorities in his nome. His appointment is often on grounds broader than party affiliation and changes in central government do not necessarily result in changes in nomarchs. Like the broader regional divisions of Greece the nomes can be traced back to the divisions of antiquity and many have developed from the classical city states.

On the local level they play an important role in the economic and social life of the country. Each unit is served by a capital town, and although these vary greatly in size and function they all act as administrative and commercial outlets for the countryside they control.

The *eparchies* are subdivisions of the nomes and number 149. In them the functions of the nomarch are carried out by his local representative. Many of the eparchies are also old divisions, but the majority retain a historical significance only. It is only in northern Greece that they have been revived as real administrative units. Further subdivisions are the municipalities and the communes, which number 256 and 5,811 respectively. According to Article 121 of the constitution the municipalities and communes are the essence of local self-government. Their sole purpose is 'the advancement of local interests and the satisfaction of the needs of the inhabitants of their area.' Each municipality is administered by the *demarchos* (mayor) and the municipal council, and each commune by its president and communal council. The president is a highly influential force in the rural communities and acts as a combination of mayor, counsellor and chairman of all community activities. The present government has allocated substantial capital sums for expenditure on projects of public benefit.

THE CIVIL SERVICE

An efficient public administration sector is an important factor in the struggle for economic development. In Greece, however, the civil service is intensely bureaucratic, productivity is low, and there is an acute lack of interest in the tasks assigned to it. The civil service modelled itself on France and adopted from the start a markedly centralised administrative system. Public authorities are mostly located in Athens, and all decisions, even minor ones, are taken by central services in the capital. The decentralisation law of 1955 failed to produce the desired results, primarily because of the shortage of competent officers to staff regional services of government departments.

Between 1956 and 1965 the numerical strength of the civil service rose from 64,956 to 89,273. The most notable increases occurred in the numbers of teachers, agricultural advisers and medical personnel. There was a particularly high increase of graduates of higher educational establishments in the civil service (65 per cent in 1965). *Prima facie,* such a highly educated staff should ensure for the service the highest degree of efficiency. Many of its inadequacies are undoubtedly a reflection of imperfections in the country's education system and there is a great need for the extension of specialised courses in administrative science. Other weaknesses stem from the absence of modern methods and equipment for the proper organisation of administrative work. Overstaffing and understaffing and disproportion in the salaries of civil servants curb incentive and produce a feeling of inferiority that is manifested in the unco-operative attitude towards the public.

Remodelling the civil service has become the prime objective of contemporary governments, but the problem of inertia still remains, and any real improvement in its structure and organisation is likely to take some considerable time.

NATIONAL DEFENCE

According to the 1968 constitution the mission of the armed forces is to defend the national independence and territorial integrity of the country and its existing political and social system against external and internal enemies. In practice the armed forces have frequently intervened in Greek internal issues, to such an extent that intervention is often accepted as an intrinsic characteristic of political life. In 1950 the Ministries of War, Marine and Military Aviation were fused into a single Ministry of National Defence. The chief of the armed forces exercises government administration and he, together with the chiefs of the army, navy and air force, is selected by the Supreme Council for National Defence.

Military service is obligatory for all males aged twenty-one and liability lasts up to the fiftieth year. The normal term of service in the active army is twenty-four months for all arms, followed by nineteen years in the first reserve and ten years in the second reserve. The normal annual contingent of recruits in peacetime is about 50,000. Every three months a quarter of the current year's contingent is called up for service.

The army was put on a regular basis soon after the declaration of Greek independence and, now thoroughly up to date, it comprises all the usual arms and corps. The total strength of the army is around 120,000. The Royal Hellenic Navy has two main bases, at Salamis near Piraeus and at Sudas Bay in Crete. It has a personnel of 1,800 officers and 16,200 ratings called up for eighteen months or enlisted. The Royal Hellenic Air Force has a strength of around 23,000 officers and men and some 260 operational aircraft.

The Greek armed forces join in large-scale exercises held within the framework of NATO. Regular officers graduate from the Military Cadet College, the Naval Cadet College, and, in the case of the Air Force, from Icarus College. Greek airmen are commonly called Icarians after the mythical Icarus—the first Greek who attempted to fly!

POLICE

The Greek police force is separated into a number of major bodies. The *Astinomia,* a body created in 1923, is responsible for the maintenance of law and order in Athens, Piraeus and Corfu, which were the largest towns and ports in the early decades of this century. The first training school for the Astinomia was at Corfu, where it was organised on English lines. The Astinomia direct traffic and assist customs officers, although the policing of coastal areas and territorial waters is the concern of the Harbour Service.

The Gendarmerie is organised and trained on a military basis and is responsible for maintaining order in the remainder of the country. In accordance with the policy of decentralisation the Gendarmerie comes under the control of the nomarch. Greece has also a security police force which, together with the military force, is unrestricted at the present time. According to many reports they have reacted fiercely to those engaged in opposition to the government.

Tourist police are located at all the country's principal vacation areas. Their duties include finding accommodation for visitors and settling disputes which may arise over hotel charges and the unfair treatment of tourists.

CURRENCY AND FINANCE

The monetary unit of Greece is the drachma, which is divided into 100 lepta. In March 1970 the us dollar was equivalent to 30.15 drachma and the pound sterling to 72.55 drachma. The Bank of Greece is the bank of issue and the government's banker. It issues notes for 1,000, 500, 100 and 50 drachma, and coins for 20, 10, 5, 2 and 1 drachma and 50, 20, 10 and 5 lepta. The Bank of Greece also supervises all the banking operations and carries out the currency committee's decisions. The latter is a body which was first set up in 1946, and consists of the Ministers of Coordination, Finance, Agriculture, Industry and Commerce, and the governor of the Bank of Greece. The function of the Committee is to lay down in broad outlines the policy to be followed at all times in the money sector, and particularly in the fields of credit, banking and foreign exchange.

The credit requirements of the farming population are met by the Agricultural Bank of Greece (established 1929), an autonomous institution with a large number of branch offices throughout the country. Housing loans are principally granted by the National Mortgage Bank of Greece, founded in 1927 as a *société anonyme*. This bank also grants loans to public corporations and public utilities as well as to the tourist industry. The commercial banks are private competitive institutions which, in addition to the usual short- and medium-term credit, provide long-term financing chiefly to industry and trade. The big commercial banks have an extensive network of branches as well as subsidiaries in some foreign countries. Branch offices of foreign banks also operate in Greece and include the Bank of America, the Chase Manhattan Bank, the First National City Bank of New York, the Bank of Nova Scotia and the American Express International Banking Corporation. In 1964 the Hellenic Industrial Development Bank was established by the merger of two former financial organisations. It is wholly State-owned and endowed with government funds. It finances industries and mining projects as well as tourist developments in the form of long-term loans and equity participation.

All Greek banks, with the exception of the Bank of Greece, and most of the other credit institutions in Greece accept deposits from individuals and companies. The maximum annual rates of interest on these accounts vary greatly, depending on the amount and duration of the deposit. Throughout the sixties Greece saw a rapid growth in the volume of private deposits and also in stock exchange transactions. In large part this is a reflection of public confidence in the national currency and the stability of the country's economy. It is a significant fact that from being a humble and unwanted currency, the drachma is today widely and officially recognised to be a hard currency on the international monetary market. In October 1969 a us economic review considered the drachma a worthy candidate for revaluation, though Greece announced that the current parity would remain unchanged.

TAXATION

Tax is payable on any income arising in Greece irrespective of a person's nationality, residence or domicile. There is no discrimination between Greek nationals and aliens. Special treaties, for example with Belgium, Cyprus, Germany, France, the uk, Italy and the us etc, ensure that taxpayers are not liable to double taxation. Foreign nationals who have resided in Greece for more than eighteen months are required on departure to produce a certificate that no taxes are outstanding.

All persons liable to taxation are required to fill an annual income return covering the preceding year and tax is then paid in ten monthly instalments from March to December on the basis of this return. Income from interest on deposits with Greek banks or branches of foreign banks operating in Greece, or interest on national bonds, is exempt from tax. Sources of income are divided into a number of categories and tax allowances vary according to the sources. For example, the allowance on income earned from salaried services amounts to 30 per cent, but may not exceed 18,000drs (£250, $600) in any one year. In the case of income from liberal professions, the deduction may reach a maximum of 25 per cent, but may not exceed 12,500drs (£170, $415). In cases where income is derived from more then one source, the net income from each source is added to form the total income and losses from one source may be offset against income from another. Business losses in particular may be offset against the profits of the following two years in the case of commercial enterprises or five years in the case of manufacturing or mining enterprises. The income of children under eighteen years of age is usually added to the father's personal income.

The following allowances may also be deducted from the total income, namely a minimum subsistence allowance of 15,000drs (£208, $500) for the taxpayer, 9,000drs (£125, $300) for the taxpayer's wife and 5,000drs (£69, $166) for each additional dependent member of the family. Allowances may also be claimed for medical expenses incurred by the family and for donations to charitable institutions. The net income remaining after these deductions is taxed at a progressive rate rising by twenty-three gradations from 2 per cent to a maximum of 49 per cent.

Since incomes are still low in comparison with western countries, the Greek government relies heavily on indirect taxation, which in 1969 was equivalent to 80.9 per cent of the total tax revenue. Because of the great variety of taxed merchandise it is difficult to give a detailed account of it here. It should be pointed out, however, that purchase tax heavily hits the lower-income groups. Imported goods are naturally expensive and are subject to both taxation and import duties. A luxury tax ranging from 10 to 300 per cent of the sale price is levied on all non-essential goods, imported or locally produced. Items coming under this tax include perfumery and cosmetics, jewellery, photographic equipment, watches, cigarette lighters, furniture, spirits and beers. Consumption tax is also levied on tobacco, public shows and high-class entertainment.

Considerable progress has been made in recent years in the modernisation of the tax system, particularly in the settlement of cases outstanding before the tax authorities. When the junta seized power some 680,000 unchecked income-tax returns, estimated at 3 million million drs, were discovered, and stiff penalties are now imposed for tax evasion, punishable by prison sentences of one to five years.

4

How They Live

IN spite of the fact that investment in housing has absorbed a high proportion of the national income and of total investment since 1961, housing conditions in Greece are extremely unsatisfactory. Throughout this century the country has been faced with a serious housing shortage, especially in the urban areas, where population increase has been most marked. According to some estimates this shortage reaches 500,000 dwellings, while other estimates put the figure much higher. The nature of the problem is clouded by extensive migration to the towns and by emigration abroad.

The greatest housing burden was posed in the 1920s and 30s when, under the terms of the Treaty of Lausanne, Greece was faced with the problem of housing refugees from Asia Minor. The government created some 1,954 new settlements, mainly in the northern provinces, and for the most part they were composed of single-storey structures of simple standard design. The cities of Athens and Salonica, however, received the brunt of the refugee population. The inhabitants of Athens increased from 292,991 in 1920 to 459,211 in 1928, of which 129,380 were refugees. The corresponding increase in Piraeus was from 133,482 to 259,659, with a refugee total of 101,185. These figures did not include the population of the suburbs of Phaleron and Kallithea, the latter having a population of over 25,000 in 1928, of which 12,516 were refugees from Asia Minor. Salonica faced similar problems. Fire devastated the city in August 1917, rendering 50,000 homeless, and the shanty town of refugees was swollen after 1923 by the influx of people from Turkey.

Under the pressure of circumstances the immigrants were encouraged to build illegally on privately owned plots, and large districts without any provision for amenities and sanitation developed around the country's main urban centres. In Athens many of these settlements were nostalgically christened with names such as New Ionia and New Smyrna, and from the outset they were little more than appalling slums. Today most of these areas have been redeveloped and some have become attractive residential districts. A few, however, continue to survive in more or less their original form and are the targets for current planning programmes.

Refugee settlement of a similar nature has continued to the present day. World War II and the civil war again brought a steady stream of refugees into the towns in search of security. At the same time the damage caused to housing as a result of the wars was enormous and there were numerous examples of villages totally destroyed. The contemporary influx, however, is a function of economic rather than political motives, and the problem of overcrowding in Greek urban centres remains intense. Where no organised development has been planned, squatting families have erected on empty plots of land small cubes of concrete and less durable structures in which to wait for the authorities to recognise them and to bring them into the municipal water and sewerage system. Athens, Salonica, Iraklion and other centres have large peripheral districts where the inhabitants live, in many cases, in conditions of extreme poverty. Of the 90,000 provincial families which settled in Athens between 1951 and 1961, 40,000 were settled in unauthorised dwellings on the margins of the built-up area. In Iraklion a continuous belt of shanty development surrounds the Venetian fortifications, the limit of the old city, and appalling conditions, even troglodytism, present acute social problems.

The following table shows the total number of substandard and overcrowded dwellings in the Athens area and in Greece as a whole in 1961.

Type of substandard dwelling	Athens	Provinces	Total (Greece)
Aged Single-Room Dwellings	45,000	180,000	225,000
Primitive Dwellings	5,000	31,000	36,400
Non-Residential Premises Used As Dwellings	17,000	23,000	40,000
Overcrowded Dwellings	68,400	247,600	316,000
Total	135,400	481,600	617,400
Per cent of total number of dwellings	27	26.5	26.6

The term slum corresponded to two categories of accommodation : primitive shelters such as temporary timber structures, tents
etc, and single-room dwellings, the majority built over thirty
years ago on the fringes of urban areas. The latter are usually
soundly constructed, but auxiliary facilities are primitive or non-
existent and their life-span is short. Greece also recognizes a
shelterless household category, comprising families living in non-
residential buildings such as basements, garages and shops, etc.
The majority of these households occupy the central areas of
cities. Thus the first three categories constitute the country's major
replacement problem. The problem of the last category (overcrowded dwellings) has been alleviated to a certain extent by the
addition, where space permits, of extra rooms. In Piraeus alone,
however, 20 per cent of all householders share dwellings, a
characteristic that becomes increasingly common in the central
areas of cities.

Until recently much of the authorised housing development in
Greece has concentrated on the provision of relatively expensive
accommodation which has intensified the problems of the under-
privileged districts. Housing activities have been mostly private
and uncoordinated. Few municipalities have built houses as they
lack the capital and proper organisation. Since 1959, and largely
in response to the demand for land, real-estate activity has grown
more rapidly than any other sector of the economy. Prices have
rocketed and investment in land, particularly near the expanding
urban centres, is still considered to be the safest form of invest-

ment. In 1963 the gross investment in housing was equivalent to 32.3 per cent of total investment in fixed assets. In 1967 the corresponding value was 29.7 per cent. The general lack of other investment outlets, and the fact that during the war the people who had invested in real estate undoubtedly fared better than those who had invested in government bonds or had savings accounts, offers some explanation of the construction boom. Another factor is the yearning of the average Greek for a home of his own. The second-home trend has also become widespread during the past decade.

In most urban centres, and especially in the Athens area, the fashion is to construct multi-storey housing units, with permissible maximum heights varying according to district. Throughout Greece as a whole some 200,000 apartment blocks were built between 1956 and 1966, and a large part of the investment has been directed into dwellings for the higher and middle-income groups. Thus Athens, and to a lesser extent Salonica, have areas where the dwellings, if on the small side, compete favourably with higher-class areas of Western Europe. A useful, if not entirely accurate, analogy would be to compare the Kolonaki quarter of Athens, near the Royal Palace, with London's Mayfair or Washington's White House district.

Such districts do not disguise the poor quality of most of the country's housing: In 1961, 47 per cent of all dwellings were not supplied with electricity, 85 per cent were without basic sanitary installations, and 71 per cent were without a mains water supply. The contrast in domestic facilities between Athens and some provincial regions in 1961 is shown in the following table.

	Greater Athens	Thrace	Epirus	Ionian Islands
Per capita consumption of electric energy (domestic use kwh.)	290	9	16	22
Shower or bath installations (percentage of households)	30	2	2	6
Drinking water installations (percentage of households)	78	21	18	20

Another unsatisfactory characteristic of Greek housing stems from the average per-room density of habitation:

Average size of dwelling and density of habitation (1961)

	Rooms per dwelling	Persons per dwelling	Persons per room
Urban areas	2.67	3.70	1.38
Semi-urban areas	2.99	4.17	1.39
Rural areas	2.73	4.33	1.59
Total Greece	2.78	4.07	1.45

The corresponding figures for the United Kingdom are an average of 4.7 rooms per dwelling and an average of 0.7 persons per room. For the United States the figures are 5.0 and 0.7 respectively. The fact that the per-room density in Athens is largely the same as for the other regions of the country is due to the rapid population increase of the city and the resultant housing shortages.

In accordance with a requirement of the 1968 constitution and the national government's plan, the securing of home ownership for a larger proportion of the Greek population is one of the basic aims of social policy. The current development programme envisages the investment of large capital sums in the public and private sectors of housing. Until recently the public housing programme amounted to only 3 per cent of total investment and had been carried out by seven different government agencies, each having their own technical and administrative staff. There is a great need for more co-operation between agencies and particularly attempts to increase the amount of comprehensive housing development. A pioneer body in this field is the Organisation for Labour Housing (OLH), which is under the control of the Ministry of Housing. More than 10,000 dwellings have already been built with the necessary public services, around 20,000 loans have been granted, and during the past few years a number of architectural and city-planning projects have been carried out, for example, at Larisa, Amalias, Corfu, Agrinion and Syra.

The problems of Greek housing can only be combated successfully when the drift of the rural population to the major urban centres is curbed. This, of course, is primarily a reflection of the economic potential of the provincial districts and involves comprehensive regional planning. An interesting scheme is now being implemented by the North of Greece Regional Development Service and concerns the transferring of the population of non-viable agricultural settlements to 122 new farming communities. This is in accordance with the government's intention to ensure full use of productive resources in every part of the country. The success of this project might well point to its further extension to other parts of Greece, thereby rejuvenating agricultural communities and counteracting the magnetic pull of the urban centres on rural life.

PRIVATE CONSUMPTION

Per-capita private consumption (at constant 1958 prices) increased from £131.20 ($314.86) in 1960 to £201 ($480.23) in 1967, giving a mean annual increase of 6.2 per cent. The percentage expenditure for 1960 and 1967 was as follows:

	1960	*1967*
Foodstuffs	40.9	36.4
Beverages	3.6	3.4
Tobacco	3.5	3.4
Clothing—footwear	11.7	14.0
Housing—water	12.8	12.9
Heating—lighting	2.9	3.4
Furniture—fittings	3.9	4.2
Current household expenses	3.2	3.2
Hygiene—personal care	3.9	3.9
Travelling—transport	5.4	6.5
Telecommunications	0.6	0.7
Recreation	6.0	7.3
Education	1.8	1.8

	1960	*1967*
Other Services	0.7	0.6
Consumption of Greeks abroad	0.7	1.0
Less: Consumption by foreigners in Greece	1.8	2.6
National private consumption	100.0	100.0

Between the two dates the rate of increase in expenditure on clothing, footwear, heating, lighting, travel and transport was particularly high. In contrast a much slower increase in expenditure characterised foodstuffs, other than meat. With the progressive trend towards the consumption of luxury, non-essential articles, the percentage domestic consumption of essential articles fell from 69.3 per cent in 1960 to 67.8 per cent in 1967.

FOOD AND DRINK

With the increase of food production and per-capita annual income, the diet of the Greek people has considerably improved in quality and quantity since 1957. Cases of serious under-nourishment have practically disappeared, although medical surveys have shown that mild specific deficiencies are not uncommon. Rickets and pellagra are rare nowadays, the latter appearing before the war in hundreds of cases yearly in northern Greece.

The food policy of the government since the end of the war was aimed at increasing intermediate animal products, such as milk, cheese and eggs. These products largely meet the protein requirements of the poorer classes, who do not often eat meat. The consumption of cereals is still high, although it has decreased in proportion with the intake of protein. The most satisfactory increases have occurred in vegetables, meat and milk, but these are still insufficient to meet requirements. Compared with some countries the Greeks have 60 per cent of cereals as the origin of their calorie intake, a proportion very much higher than the countries of Western Europe, with the exception of Spain,

Portugal and Italy. The average daily calorie intake is about 2,500 a person compared with over 3,000 in the United States.

In 1967 the Greeks spent £77.40 ($185.84) a head on food and drink. This was equivalent to 39.8 per cent of the total individual private consumption. The expenditure on specific food items is shown in the following table:

	£	$	Average annual rate of growth 1960-7
Bread and cereals	8.94	21.46	1.8
Meat	13.95	33.50	3.9
Fish	4.22	10.13	4.7
Dairy produce	12.27	29.46	5.8
Fats	6.31	15.16	0.4
Vegetables and fruit	18.54	44.50	4.6
Refreshments	1.50	3.60	6.6
Sugar and confectionery	4.63	11.13	4.0
Other foodstuffs	0.50	1.20	2.6
Beverages	6.54	15.70	4.4
Total	77.40	185.84	3.8

The above figures, it should be stressed, are national averages and, although there has been a considerable improvement in the diet of the general population, there are certain parts of the country, chiefly the mountainous districts, where nutrition continues to be poor. In many rural communities the staple diet remains bread, potatoes, rice, vegetables and fruit. Meat, mainly chicken and lamb, is eaten on special days, but beef is regarded as a luxury. Goat's cheese is the most characteristic dairy product. Since 1959 the UN Food and Agriculture Organisation has been active in promoting improved diets among the rural population.

Greek menus and dishes are more varied and sophisticated in urban areas; within the non-urban population a distinction can be made between inland and coastal settlements, the diet of the latter comprising variable amounts of seafood. In the cities breakfast is usually a light meal of bread, jam or honey and

F

coffee, taken from 6.30am onwards. Lunch is usually taken around 1.00pm and dinner not before 8.30, or even later in the larger centres.

Normally a Greek meal begins with a spaghetti (macaroni) or rice dish with tomato or meat sauce. Alternatives are soup or *hor d'œuvres.* This is followed by a meat or fish course but beef and veal tend to be plentiful only in the larger centres. Pork is usually good where obtainable, but mutton and lamb are the most common meat dishes and are prepared in an infinite variety of ways. Chicken is nearly always obtainable and in coastal areas the choice of fish can include mullet, sprat, octopus, squid, mussels, prawns, crayfish and lobster.

A number of the more sophisticated dishes of the cities have reached the tables of western countries, particularly *moussaka,* a pie consisting of layers of potato and aubergine or marrow, alternating with mincemeat; and *dolmadhes,* rolls of rice and meat in vine leaves cooked in olive oil. A great variety of sweet dishes is available, with a strongly oriental character that evokes the Ottoman taste. Among the most popular are *baclava,* layered pastry filled with honey, nuts and spices, *kataifi,* shredded wheat filled with sweetened nuts and spices, and *galaktoboureko,* pastry filled with vanilla custard and cinnamon. A Greek meal generally ends with a fruit course and most main dishes are eaten with a green salad.

The Greeks are, as a whole, a temperate people. They are proud of their water, which is often considered the greatest delicacy and forms an integral part of every meal. Wines fall into the resinated and non-resinated varieties : the former, *retsina,* perpetuate an ancient tradition whereby the 3 per cent of resin was at first added for preservation, then becoming an acquired taste. In rural areas almost every family owns a small vineyard and each village has a grape press where the farmers make their own *retsina.* Famous non-resinated wines are produced in Crete, Thera, Paros, Samos and Achaea. Beer is of good quality, but expensive, and resembles the European lager beers—in fact the best-known brewery, *Fix,* was begun by a compatriot of the Bavarian King Otho. *Ouzo* is the spirit of the country, a drink flavoured with anise and commonly diluted with water; it is usually accompanied by a plate of *mezedes* (*hors d'œuvres*) consisting of small pieces of fried liver, sardines, olives, fish roe, egg, tomato, cucumber, etc. In both town and country to offer the visitor something to eat and drink is a traditional gesture of hospitality: it can vary from a piece of cake to a spoonful of preserves or a piece of Turkish (Greek) delight, accompanied by *ouzo* or coffee and a glass of water. Oriental coffee is prepared in a number of ways, but European varieties, including the instant ones, are greatly increasing in popularity.

CLOTHES

In 1967, Greeks spent an average of £27.25 ($65.40) per head on clothing (including footwear). The corresponding figure for 1960 was £15.60 ($37.46), so that the average annual increase rate between the two dates was 8.4 per cent. The rapid growth of the country's cities and their 'westernisation' has meant that the urban dweller has become more fashion-conscious and the character of the domestic textile and clothing industries is adapting itself accordingly. There is, of course, a wide gulf between town and country, but even in the villages urban-style clothes are quickly replacing the traditional peasant dress with its strong regional character. This exchange of ideas is a two-way process, for the traditional designs and fabrics of rural Greece are now appearing in the international *haute-couture* salons, earning admiration for the Greek fashion world.

The city women, particularly the Athenians, are exceptionally fashionable, though the style of dress is fairly casual. A hat is a rarity, and no one wears gloves in spring or summer, largely because of the Greek climate. Fashion consciousness does not end with women: in Athens tailoring is a highly developed craft and men's tailors compete in style and workmanship with their counterparts in Western Europe. Tailored shirts are also of high quality and the shoemaking craft is geared to the Athenian male's passion for fashionable and quality footwear.

SOCIAL INSURANCE

A multiplicity of social insurance organisations exist in Greece which offer protection for the working population against the risks of old age, illness, maternity, disability and death. At present, 95 per cent of the total population is covered by the 338 main and auxiliary insurance funds in operation. Many of the smaller organisations which cover special categories of the working population belong to the formative years of the country's social insurance evolution. The major weaknesses of the general system, especially the unequal insurance coverage of the population, has resulted in a number of recent reforms, and an anticipated merger of social insurance funds into a limited number of large organisations. The new social security code will govern the entire field of social protection, with comprehensive rules.

The IKA (Social Security Fund) is the general, national agency for main social insurance and is the largest organisation in the country. It covers private salaried workers and wage-earners, except those insured by other professional categories of main insurance agencies. IKA began operation in 1937, at which time it took over protection of wage and salary earners in Athens, Piraeus and Salonica. Its coverage was later extended by stages to those employed in all urban centres throughout the country. The upheavals of World War II upset the foundation of IKA, but it regained financial stability with the result that, today, approximately 200 branch offices, manned by an administrative staff of 5,200, are in operation. The number of persons who come under IKA insurance total approximately 950,000. If the 200,000 persons on its pension roll and the dependents of its members and pensioners are added, then the total number of persons covered by IKA amounts to 2,300,000 or 27 per cent of the population.

Two branches of insurance function at present within IKA: the pensions branch and the sickness and maternity branch. Its revenue is derived from contributions from the insured workers themselves and from their employers and these are charged as a percentage of earnings up to a maximum of 6,000 drs a month (£83, $199). The general proportions payable are 17 per cent by the employer and 9.5 per cent by the insured person, but there is some variation throughout the country, for in Athens and Piraeus the employer contributes 18 per cent and the worker 9.5 per cent. In the remainder of continental Greece and in Euboea charges are reduced by 10 per cent and in the islands (excluding Euboea) by 20 per cent. Old-age pensions are paid to men and women at the ages of 65 and 60 respectively, though in certain instances they may be granted at a younger age. The pension payable is determined by the number of years of the insured person's employment and also by the amount of his contributions.

Until relatively recently the agrarian population of Greece was excluded from insurance protection. Since 1961 farmers have enjoyed insurance cover afforded by OGA (Organisation for Farmers' Insurance) and this also includes coastal fishermen and tradesmen and artisans of small villages, a total of more than 4 million persons. OGA is also steadily extending its protection to the fruits of the farmer's labour—insurance of anticipated agricultural income against unforeseen risks such as damage to crops from hail and frost. OGA provides pensions to all farmers (male and female) on reaching the age of 65. Initially it paid old-age pensions only, but from November 1967 sickness and accident relief have been included. The new increased rates of farmers' pensions introduced in 1967 amount, according to each case, to £4 ($10) per head when the beneficiary has no family obligations, and £5.5 ($13) or £6.6 ($16), for those whose wife is aged under or over 65 years respectively. OGA has been regarded by many as a model insurance organisation, operating on the principle of maximum decentralisation. It is one of the few Greek institutions lacking in bureacracy, operating with a minimum of staff, and it has brought speedy and effective services to farmers. Civil servants and members of the armed forces are insured by the State against risks such as those covered by IKA.

HEALTH AND MEDICAL SERVICES

Today, the average life expectancy of the Greek population compares favourably with western countries, averaging 67.3 years for males, compared with 68 years in England and Wales, 66.7 in West Germany and 67 in the United States. This, however, is not so much due to the efficiency of health and medical services as to other factors such as diet, climate and natural longevity. The infant death rate has improved since 1950 (when the rate was 34.4 per 1,000 live births) but it still remains high, as does the death rate from infectious diseases. Although intensive campaigns have been carried out against diphtheria, malaria and tuberculosis, morbidity from these and other diseases still remains high.

A major problem in the effective running of medical and health services lies in the unequal distribution of qualified staff. In 1961 Greece had 13,153 doctors, 50 per cent of whom practised in Greater Athens and 66 per cent of the remainder in Salonica, Patras, Volos and in other large towns. Thus, in Athens, the ratio of inhabitants per doctor was 305 compared with 1,360 in the Peloponnesus, 1,576 in Epirus and 3,293 in Thrace, etc. Hospital accommodation presents the same picture. In 1965 there were 1,045 hospitals and clinics, 258 being located in Athens, which had 25,725 out of a total of 45,288 available beds. Many of the provincial hospitals are extremely small units and this often prevents the use of complicated and expensive equipment for modern treatment. The transfer of provincial patients to Athens for hospitalisation greatly increases the economic and social cost of the health service. It is still common for Greeks who can afford it to seek medical treatment in other European countries, and Britain is naturally attractive.

The value of social insurance in Greece is particularly important when it comes to medical treatment, which generally is not free; in certain cases a lifetime's savings can be spent on it. The 74 state general hospitals (with 8,216 beds) do examine and treat, mostly free of charge, patients who are either indigent or of modest means, but an adequate number of beds is reserved for patients who can afford to pay for treatment and for those who are covered by the various social insurance organisations.

IKA clients receive medical attention through the dispensaries and laboratories owned by IKA as well as by IKA doctors who treat patients at their private practices. The total IKA medical staff consists of over 3,300 doctors and 2,000 nurses. Hospitalisation is provided by hospitals, clinics and sanatoria which are under contract to IKA and also by four hospitals owned by IKA. Auxiliary medical care is also provided by IKA and covers mainly the supply of therapeutic equipment and special treatments such as X-rays.

On the preventive side IKA services cover the medical supervision of expectant mothers and infant care, carried out through district medical centres or by nurses visiting the homes of the insured. In addition, there is special protection for invalid and abnormal children, and young children of working mothers can be cared for in children's playgrounds. In cases of sickness and maternity IKA pays cash allowances amounting to 50 per cent of the insured person's salary, although this is often increased by a proportion corresponding to family burdens. It is paid up to a duration of 84 days in cases of maternity, 180 in cases of sickness and 360 in the particular case of tuberculosis.

In the rural areas persons insured or in receipt of pensions from OGA, and the members of their families, are entitled to full medical and hospital treatment. This is administered through a network of rural health units—1,390 dispensaries and 98 health stations served by 1,282 and 101 medical staff respectively. Each health station has a strength of six, ten or fifteen beds, a staff of one or two physicians, and an equal number of midwives, nurses and administrative staff. For more serious cases the patients are taken to the nearest state hospital or to Athens or Salonica. More than 300,000 persons insured with OGA receive full hospital treatment each year in their own right.

CARE OF THE OLD AND DISABLED

Family life, especially in rural Greece, is a closely-knit organisation and care of the old does not present the pressing problems common to Britain and the USA. The majority of Greeks willingly care for aged parents, both as an act of genuine affection and a duty; this, at times, can be a matter of extreme sacrifice, especially if the aged are not covered by any insurance system. Proposals for special grants in such conditions have been advocated by a number of governments. Perhaps another reason for keeping aged relatives within the confines of the family unit is the present standard of old people's institutions, many of which fail to satisfy modern social demands.

The situation is worse in relation to homes for the incurable. It is estimated that 10,000 chronically sick live with their families. Greece has also an estimated 16,000 blind, 8-9,000 deaf and dumb and around 35,000 cripples. Social interest in the assistance and rehabilitation of the handicapped is manifest mainly in private activity. The existing institutions are not adequate to cover present needs and neither do they offer complete assistance, lacking training schools, specialist staff and concern for the placement of the handicapped in jobs.

In conclusion, Greece has a long way to go in the organisation and improvement of its welfare services, although, annually, significant steps forward are being made. It must be remembered that after World War II little progress was possible until the early fifties, and then the country's main objective was the revitalisation of the economy. Greece now realises that an advance in social welfare has favourable effects on productivity, and comprehensive programmes for improvement are being implemented. The shortage of suitably qualified personnel for welfare units is extreme, and bridging this gap is both technically and financially difficult. New schools and training centres are being established, and at the same time research into the social needs of various parts of the country and groups of the population is proceeding apace.

5

How They Work

In 1950 the Greek economy was in a desperate state. The combined effects of World War II and the civil war left an aftermath of poverty and distress. Hundreds of settlements were destroyed, mines and factories were abandoned, and road, rail and port installations completely disrupted. The great problem of economic and social rehabilitation was faced with courage and determination, and with generous foreign aid, particularly from the United States, the programmes for reconstruction and stabilisation have transformed the life of the country.

Greece still belongs to the general category of developing countries with one of the lowest gross national products in Europe, but most sectors of the economy have experienced an impressively high growth rate within the last decade. Measures to modernise agriculture, promote industrialisation and raise income levels generally are both numerous and complex. Corresponding developments in communications and energy production, factors of basic importance to the economic advancement of the country as a whole, have similarly made substantial progress.

As in nearly all developing countries, agriculture is the most important sector of the economy, in 1965 directly supporting 53 per cent of the total population. It furthermore provided 27 per cent of the gross national product and represented two-thirds of the country's merchandise exports. The following table shows the structure of the economically active population (male and female) in 1965.

	Employment (in thousand persons)	Percentage distribution
Agriculture, forests, fisheries	1,855	53.0
Mining and quarrying	23	0.7
Manufacturing	459	13.1
Public utilities	26	0.7
Construction	187	5.3
Transport and communications	167	4.8
Commerce, banking, insurance	300	8.6
Other services (including armed services)	484	13.8
Total	3,501	100.0

In spite of its important role in the Greek economy, agriculture remains inefficient. Its rate of growth has lagged far behind that of manufacturing industry, whose economic indicator (1959 = 100) rose from 157.3 in 1965 to 189.4 in 1967. Marked inequalities have now arisen between the agricultural and non-agricultural sectors. In 1965 the agricultural per-capita income was 36 per cent of the corresponding income of the manufacturing sector and about 51 per cent of the national average. Adding to this problem is the fact that industry shows an overwhelming concentration in the Athens-Piraeus area, which has important locational advantages, including the presence of a large urban market. In 1961 the Athens area accounted for 50.4 per cent of the total number of industrial and manufacturing establishments and 54.8 per cent of the total population employed in industry. Since this date, and in spite of industrial decentralisation policies, Athens' percentage share of industrial establishments has continued to rise.

The development problem in Greece, therefore, is twofold. Not only is there a marked and growing disparity in income levels between the rural and urban areas, but there are also inequalities between the metropolitan area and the rest of the country. Stated more bluntly, the problem is that of an advanced Athens versus a more backward Greece, and an OECD report for 1965 classifies the remainder of the country as 'lagging or underdeveloped regions.'

It is only relatively recently that Greece has embarked upon comprehensive development programmes, and these have been seriously disrupted by the country's unstable political environment. The first major official undertaking was a general five-year programme for the 1960-4 period. Its objective was the gradual removal of disparities among the regions, but few concrete suggestions were put forward to achieve this. In 1965 the draft of the 'Five-Year Economic Development Plan (1966-70)' appeared and its strictly defined policy measures were adjusted to those of the European Economic Community. Political upheavals resulted in few implementations of the proposals and a revision and updating duly produced the 'Five-Year Development Programme (1968-72).'

In essence these national development programmes emphasised the need for a balanced, self-supporting and prosperous Greek economy, and one in which the country's resource potential is utilised to its fullest possible extent. It is encouraging to note that great emphasis is being given to the preservation of the country's unique cultural heritage and exceptionally beautiful natural environment, both of which play major roles in the tourist industry. The current programme stresses the speeding-up of the rate of productivity growth, especially in agriculture, which is scheduled to increase by 5.6 per cent per annum.

AGRICULTURE

The problems involved in placing Greek agriculture on a competitive basis are immeasurable. Out of a total area of 32,553,805 acres, only 9,326,348 acres (28 per cent) are classified as arable. Even here the definition includes much land of low quality, as well as fallow that has been uncultivated for up to four or five years. Slope and altitude greatly restrict cultivation, and farming in many areas has extended beyond the limits consistent with conservational land use. Even in Macedonia and Thessaly the extensive reclamation projects have virtually exhausted the limits of further cultivation. Elsewhere, the most productive arable land occurs in a series of discontinuous coastal plains or in higher interior plains in mountainous districts.

Climatic influences are also restrictive, and one of the major difficulties is the shortage of water, especially during the summer when totals are low and the evaporation rate high. Rainfall totals are irregular from year to year, and large areas of limestone and porous subsoils hinder the construction of storage dams. In 1965 only 1,334,000 acres, or 14.5 per cent of the land under cultivation, were irrigated. Although this figure was a marked improvement on the 1958 figure of 963,700 acres, the irrigated area is still small in view of the fact that official estimates indicate that the water potential of the country is sufficient for the irrigation of 45 per cent of the present cultivated area.

Another factor limiting agriculture is the poor, and for the the most part exhausted, soil which is the product of centuries of misuse and mismanagement. Soil erosion is widespread and Plato's description of the soils of Attica as 'the bones of a body wasted away with disease' applies to large sections of the country today. One of the main causes of soil erosion is overstocking, particularly with goats. In 1967 there were over 3 million goats in Greece, a figure far too large for the 3.7 to 5 million acres which are available as permanent grazing. In addition there were over six million sheep.

Greece, therefore, has the lowest agricultural land per-capita values in the Balkans. Regionally it varies from above 24 acres per head of rural population in parts of northern and central Greece to below 1.2 acres in parts of Epirus, the Peloponnesus and the islands. The resultant population pressure on available agricultural land is further intensified by the existence of traditional inheritance laws, which lead to the subdivision of the farmed area into small, privately owned holdings consisting of a number of scattered plots. The fragmentation is greatest in Crete, where each farmer has an average of 12.7 plots per holding : it has been estimated that the average walking time for a Cretan farmer is ten minutes to his nearest plots and ninety minutes to his farthest. This, together with the low level of technology, is a principal factor causing low productivity—both in yields per acre and per worker employed. Through legislation and other methods, contemporary governments have attempted to discourage those factors which contribute to fragmentation, for example dowry and inheritance laws.

Cultivation is still predominantly concerned with tilled field crops such as wheat, tobacco and cotton. Vine-growing, although more limited than in the past, is traditional and in some regions is the sole undertaking. In the Peloponnesus and Crete, Corinth currants and sultana raisins respectively, provide the main source of income for a large proportion of the rural population. The olive is also a traditional crop, the olive harvest greatly influencing total annual agricultural income. In recent years the cultivation of citrus and other fruits has expanded and from the income standpoint they have tended to replace vines. A permanent problem confronting agricultural policy is the tenacity with which the farming community persists with some traditional crops such as wheat and tobacco; for a number of years the wheat crop has exceeded domestic requirements, and although large amounts are exported the government has had to purchase it in bulk at artificially high prices. This throws a heavy burden on the national budget. Tobacco production presents a similar problem, over-production creating disposal difficulties in a world market congested with tobacco of the oriental type. Through incentives and subsidies agricultural policy has been directed at inducing farmers to turn part of their acreage over to other crops, such as cotton, fodder and citrus fruits.

Experts who have studied the problems of Greek agriculture are agreed that improvement is best tackled through a number of major channels. The most significant of these are changes in the organisational and institutional bases of farming, in particular the modernisation of agricultural co-operatives to which the majority of Greek farmers belong, improvements in crop and animal yields through the use of better varieties, a more intensive use of fertilisers, a speeding-up of mechanisation and land-reclamation schemes, and the extension of an intensified programme of agricultural research and education. Substantial improvements in each of these measures have been made since the early 1960s although the basic problems still remain. The nature of this improvement, however, varies between the regions, with Macedonia and Thessaly being the most agriculturally advanced.

In spite of the great difficulties facing agricultural improvement, production has substantially increased since 1954 and, in general, farmers have been turning to wider markets. The progress in output between 1954-5 and 1968-9 is revealed in the following table; figures are for thousand metric tons:

Product	1954-5	1968-9
Wheat	1,293	1,633
Barley	299	504
Rice	74	106
Tobacco	82	74
Cotton	159	255
Sugar beet	–	857
Currants	70	87
Sultanas	40	92
Table grapes	120	207
Olives (oil)	108	152
Citrus fruit	196	500
Apples, peaches and pears	92	422
Potatoes	432	685

The increased yields are due largely to an expansion in the financing of the agricultural sector and to improvements in road network, telecommunications and electrification which have contributed decisively to the growing unification of the rural and urban areas. Yet, despite the uninterrupted growth of agricultural output and the switch to new and more market-orientated crops, agriculture has gradually lost ground to other sectors of the economy. Its share in the formation of the gross national product has declined in comparison with industry and services.

LIVESTOCK

The livestock sector of Greek farming has been the object of a special study. Production has expanded substantially in recent years but it is still unable to meet domestic requirements. Greece imports £62.5 ($150) million worth of meat and dairy produce annually, and the rate is increasing, reflecting the rise in the standard of living and the growing number of tourists. Most of the red-meat imports have been frozen beef from South America, lamb and mutton from Australia and New Zealand, and some chilled beef from Yugoslavia.

In order to check rapidly increasing foreign-exchange expenditure and develop its own livestock industry the Ministers of Commerce and Industry approved a plan in 1969 to import 720 head of cattle for replacement purposes from the United States. These were maintained for three months at the American Farm School in Salonica. The government has also encouraged commercial-sized production units to take the place of the traditional small farms, and is developing a programme for improving large areas of unused or under-used land for grazing purposes.

Poultry farming has increased rapidly, especially between 1965 and 1967 when output rose by 75.6 per cent. The comparatively high cost of production, however, has led to competition from imported frozen produce, and corrective tariffs have been imposed to protect domestic production.

FORESTRY

Greek forests underwent widespread damage during the last war and the ensuing internal strife. At the time of the 1961 census the area covered by forests was around 6 million acres, which represented 18 per cent of the total area of the country. The output of forestry products represented 3.2 per cent of total primary production. Three-quarters of the forest area is covered by timber suitable for construction purposes, the remainder being of low growth and small economic value. The state owns 65.5 per cent of the forests, around 15 per cent belong to monasteries and other institutions, and the remainder is privately owned.

In 1961, Macedonia produced 30.3 per cent of the total forestry output, followed by Central Greece and Euboea with 18.7 per cent, the Peloponnesus with 15.4 per cent, Thessaly with 15 per cent, Epirus with 8.2 per cent, Thrace with 6.9 per cent, and Island Greece with 5.5 per cent.

Re-afforestation is taking place, and between 1961 and 1967 a further 86,487 acres were planted. The main forestry products are building timber (which fails to meet domestic requirements), wood for fuel and charcoal (which is decreasing owing to the substitution of more economical fuels) and resin. Resin production fluctuates with changes in the demand and price; in 1967 it amounted to 22,980 tons.

FISHERIES

During the post-war period the output of fisheries increased from 33,600 tons in 1948 to 95,500 tons in 1964; that is, at a rate of 7.4 per cent per annum. Of the 1964 production, 7,500 tons came from the Mediterranean fisheries, 53,000 from the Aegean and Ionian seas, 14,000 from coastal fisheries and 21,000 from the Atlantic. The number of inhabitants who make a living from fishing is estimated at 52,900 (1964) and income from fishing represents less than 1 per cent of the gross national income. In recent years governments have made efforts to organise fishing by the construction of special quays with refrigerator installations at the principal fishing ports.

A traditional activity of Greek islanders is sponge fishing; this has suffered from the manufacture of synthetic sponges and is declining in volume. In 1967 there were 89 sponge fishing craft which employed a total of 726 crew and divers, and production amounted to 137,270lb.

MINERAL RESOURCES

The share of the mining sector in the gross domestic product is very small, approximating to 1.3 per cent. It is important to stress, however, that knowledge of the country's mineral deposits is still limited, and only recently has any systematic study of it been undertaken. In spite of the fact that several basic metallurgical units have been established, the country's mining industry is still geared mainly to exporting ore in a raw state.

The limited hydro-electric possibilities of Greece and the lack of other indigenous fuel have necessitated the development of lignite deposits for electrical generation and other uses. In addition to major lignite fields at Aliverion and Ptolemais, exploitation is also undertaken at Megalopolis in the central Peloponnesus, where there are deposits totalling many hundred million tons. Ultimately this will lead to a substantial increase in power resources. Iron ore (containing 40-50 per cent iron), mostly of the haematite and limonite category, is considered to be limited but is beginning to reduce the volume of ore imports for the expanding domestic iron and steel industry. Deposits of chromiferous ores are, on the contrary, estimated at tens of millions of tons. Other minerals include chromite, zinc, lead, copper, pyrites and magnesite. Aluminium plants are based on the country's bauxite deposits, and a modern asbestos mine at Kozani is planned to produce 20,000 tons of asbestos fibre annually, mainly for the export market.

MANUFACTURING INDUSTRY

It is often remarked that there are almost as many industrial concerns in Greece as there are people engaged in industry! Small artisans' workshops, reminiscent of oriental bazaars, and numerous small shops run by craftsmen are still huddled together in some streets of Athens and other principal cities, but

G

artisan manufacturing, characterised by handicraft methods of production, is geographically dispersed throughout the country. It covers approximately half the total manpower employed in manufacturing. A concentration of small-sized firms is found in clothing, footwear, wood and furniture, metal processing, food, beverages and some lines of chemical production. There has even been a revival in this kind of industry, particularly in the manufacturing of Greek articles likely to attract tourists; for example, handwoven goods, embroideries, light furniture, ceramics, and leather and metal goods. In 1966 the Committee for Workshop Credit approved the terms and conditions whereby loans are granted to small production units. The aim is to promote modernisation, increase productivity and develop new markets at home and abroad.

A significant characteristic of Greek manufacturing industry today is the existence of small-scale concerns alongside large modern factories and plants which reflect the country's substantial achievement in industrialisation. In 1965, however, only forty firms employed a working force of 500 persons and over, giving a combined total of 45,028 workers. Government policy in the past has favoured the concentration of industrial activity in the main urban areas, particularly in Athens-Piraeus, which is the country's only real industrial area by western standards.

Legislation in 1965 provided for the establishment of industrial zones in Salonica, Patras, Volos, Kavalla and Iraklion, and minor industrial zones are envisaged for the towns of Kalamata, Ioannina, Larisa and Chalkis. The creation of such zones is aimed at promoting regional development, and a whole series of incentives in the form of tax exemptions has been established to promote industrial decentralisation. A successful industrial complex has been developed a few miles west of Salonica. An oil refinery is in operation, with pipelines to modern facilities for unloading tankers in the Thermaic Gulf. Petrochemicals, an ammonia plant, a steam cracker and various chemical industries form integrated plants, together with a steel mill with a projected annual capacity of 300,000 metric tons.

MAJOR INDUSTRIAL UNDERTAKINGS

In 1954 the most important industries were food, beverages, tobacco, clothing and footwear, which accounted for 62.5 per cent of the manufacturing product. Since 1961 there has been a relative decrease in their importance, due to substantial investment in other branches of industry, but they can still be regarded as leading industries. The textile industry in particular has witnessed the introduction of highly modernised mills, for example cotton spinning in Volos. The following table shows the progress realised between 1954 and 1968 and the change in the composition of the manufacturing product:

Branches	*1954*	*1968*
Food, beverages and tobacco	28.0	21.2
Textiles	16.2	14.4
Clothing and footwear	18.3	12.1
Wood products and furniture	4.7	4.4
Paper, printing and publishing	3.9	4.7
Chemicals and allied trades	6.1	12.9
Stone, clay and glass	6.0	8.2
Basic metal industries	0.9	4.0
Metal manufactures, engineering and electrical goods	10.9	11.3
Transport equipment	2.4	4.5
Other manufacturing	2.6	2.3
Total	100.0	100.0

More clearly than anything else, however, the extent to which Greek firms have succeeded in penetrating into foreign markets reveals how far the country has travelled on the road to industrialisation. In 1958 exports of manufactured goods amounted to no more than £2 ($5) million and represented only 2.1 per cent of total export earning, whereas in 1969 the corresponding figures were £75 ($177) million and 33.5 per cent. This indicates that a growing number of branches of manufacturing industry are gradually acquiring the ability to compete under international conditions.

Important developments have been the setting up of sugar refineries, the first of which went into production at Larisa in 1962. It was followed by the Platy refinery (1963) and the Serres refinery (1964). The gradual reduction of sugar imports has thus become possible, and its reflection on agriculture can be seen in the increase from 15,800 acres devoted to sugar beet in 1962 to 39,784 acres in 1965.

Heavy investment in the country's shipbuilding is already leading to a change in the structure of employment. Hellenic Shipyards started in 1958, setting up the first large modern shipyard for the repair and construction of ships, at Skaramanga, near Athens. This firm is the largest single employer of industrial labour in Greece and had 4,313 workers in 1968. In 1969 the Eleusis Shipyards were inaugurated which, during their initial stage of operation, will undertake ship repairs and refitting. It is firmly believed that shipbuilding and ship-repairing can develop into one of the main branches of Greek manufacturing, with especially favourable effects on the country's balance of payments.

The first marked rise in output from basic metallurgical industries occurred in 1964 and 1965, with the establishment of blast furnaces at Halivourghiki, near Athens. In 1968 they employed a total of 1,320 workers. With the opening in 1966 of the Greek Aluminium Company at Aspra Spitia in Boeotia, Greece acquired her largest metallurgical plant and largest exporting industrial concern. Based on the country's bauxite deposits, the complex includes harbour installations, alumina, electrode and aluminium factories, together with two housing estates complete with schools, sports grounds and a medical and commercial centre. In 1968 it employed 904 workers and it carries out the entire process of converting bauxite into aluminium.

Other major investments have taken place in the petroleum industry. In 1959 a State refinery was set up at Aspropyrgos, followed by the Esso-Pappas refinery near Salonica which began operations in 1966. Greece's first motor-tyre factory was set up by Pirelli in Patras and began production in 1962. The chemical industry has also achieved substantial progress, and new factories at Ptolemais and Salonica make Greece self-supporting in nitrogen and phosphate fertilisers.

Co-operation between Greek and foreign capital and entrepreneurial experience has been the cornerstone in the creation of these large industrial complexes. The major role is played by private enterprise against a background of State support and assistance, and the latter has been active in strengthening incentives and facilities, especially to foreign investment capital.

POWER

The industrial progress of Greece would not have been possible without systematic efforts, still continuing, to carry out a large-scale electrification programme. This has been based on exploitation of the country's lignite deposits and water-power resources, and production and distribution are the responsibility of the Public Power Corporation. At the end of 1952 the production of electricity was based almost entirely on thermal units operating on imported fuel. Installed capacity amounted to about 230 MW, compared with the present capacity of 2,315 MW. Consumption has risen from 670m kWh in 1952 to 7,603m kWh in 1969, but the cost of energy is still high and the policies of contemporary governments have stressed the need for utilising all available water power and lignite coal reserves.

Significant hydro-electric projects include Ladon (70 MW), Kremasta (437 MW), Kastrakion (320 MW), Tavropas (130 MW), Louros (10 MW) and Agra (50 MW), with others under completion at Edessa (19 MW) and Polyphytos (360 MW). Large thermal power plants are located at Ptolemais (320 MW), Megalopolis (250 MW), Aliverion (480 MW) and Athens-Piraeus (640 MW). This substantial development in electrical energy has provided a basis for industrialisation and for the rise in social standards throughout Greece. The extension of electric power to rural areas is continuing to make progress.

TOURISM

The tourist industry plays a major role in the economic life of Greece. Throughout the post-war period it has built itself up into an industry with foreign exchange rates amounting to one-third of the total value of Greek exports. In 1967 the tourist trade earned £53 ($126.8) million and these receipts, together with other invisible earnings, help to finance Greece's heavy volume of imports, effectively closing the trade gap with a number of countries.

Greece experienced a considerable influx of tourists after the devaluation of the drachma in 1963, and the average annual increase in tourist traffic for the period 1954-63 was 17.3 per cent. 1966 marked a record year for the industry, with official statistics giving a total of 1,131,730 arrivals, an increase of 13.7 per cent on 1965. The increase in the tourist traffic in that year exceeded the average international rate, which was given as 10 per cent. American nationals headed the list (20 per cent), followed by West Germans (12), British (11), French (10), Scandinavians (9.6) and Italians (7).

The slowing down of tourist traffic in 1967-8 can be attributed to a slight decline in economic growth and private consumption in Western Europe and to a number of political issues in the eastern Mediterranean—the Arab-Israeli War, the Greek-Turkish crisis over Cyprus, and the Greek military *coup*. In 1969 the number of arrivals had again risen to over one million.

Undoubtedly a significant factor in the increasing popularity of Greece as a vacation centre is its low cost of living. The further advantages the country offers the tourist in terms of climate, scenery and tangible manifestations of ancient civilisations need not be stressed. Government authorities over the years have launched many an ambitious tourist development programme. At present, under the auspices of the Greek Tourist

Organisation, special emphasis is being given to the infrastructure of the industry, and substantial investment in hotel accommodation, general amenities and personnel training has taken place. Athens is the major tourist centre, and in 1969 accounted for 44.1 per cent of the total accommodation capacity in higher-grade hotels and 26.9 per cent in remaining categories. Modern hotels, however, and private activity in the tourist field, are making a great impact in provincial Greece.

LABOUR RELATIONS AND WORKING CONDITIONS

Greek workers enjoy the full protection of the State, and all matters concerning the labour force are the responsibility of the Ministry of Labour. Workers are engaged through the local government employment agencies at which all unemployed persons are required to register. This procedure, however, is merely a formality, as the employer is free to engage any person of his choice, provided the latter is on the registers of the local agency. The employment of aliens is subject to a special work permit from the Ministry of Labour.

Labour laws cover persons employed in industry, offices, commerce and hotels, but many of the laws are old and are complicated by many alterations made to meet changing requirements. Legislation lays down minimum standards of health and safety in all wage-earning employment, but the many small workshops mean that the problems of enforcement remain paramount. In theory children up to the age of 14 may not be employed and children between 14 and 16 must pass a medical examination and may be employed only in certain kinds of work.

The normal working day consists of eight hours, six days a week, but special regulations provide shorter hours for office staff of industrial concerns, banks, etc. Overtime may be worked in special cases if approved by the Ministry of Labour, the rate of pay for up to 60 hours per annum being the standard rate plus 50 per cent. Persons employed on night shift, between

10pm and 6am, are entitled to pay at the standard rate plus 25 per cent. For work on Sundays and public holidays 75 per cent above the standard rate is payable.

Holiday entitlements vary, but, in general, salaried employees of personal firms and partnerships receive at least eight continuous working days' holiday in each calendar year, and wage earners at least six days. To these are added one day for each six months' service (over and above the first year), up to a maximum of 18 days for salaried staff and 12 days for other employees.

Collective bargaining has been encouraged by various laws for the past fifty years. Under a law passed in 1955 collective agreements are concluded and signed by representatives of both employers and employees, and terms of employment and general conditions of work are established. In the event of failure to reach agreement, the dispute is settled by arbitration tribunals of first or second instance, in which both employers' and workers' organisations are represented. The terms agreed either by collective labour agreement or by decision of the tribunals are legally and automatically binding unless an individual employee has negotiated more favourable terms.

Social insurance institutions, in which all persons in private employment are compulsorily insured, were discussed in Chapter 4. The organisations are legal entities and operate in accordance with the provisions of a special law. The benefits provided are for pensions, sickness (or confinement), accident, unemployment and call-up allowances. If an employee, engaged for an unspecified period, and having completed six months' service, is called up for military service, the employer is required to reinstate him on discharge and retain him for at least one year from the date of his re-engagement.

TRADE UNIONS

The history of trade unionism in Greece has been a troubled one. The General Confederation of Trade Unions was created in 1918 and represented the amalgamation of 214 unions with 60,000 members. At this period, however, a total of 336 small unions existed with over 100,000 members. The control of trade unions by the government in earlier decades of the century meant that workers never managed to overcome the institutional obstructions that made genuine representation impossible. In principle trade unionism was free, but an elaborate system of representation has often been organised to exclude the possibility of a radical labour leadership. The official attitude towards strikes was also severe. Although the constitution recognised strikes as a right of the worker, a Metaxist law giving the government the authority for political conscription of strikers was often applied, thereby transforming the strike into a criminal act. The same effect resulted from another law passed in 1955, which forbade strikes after the Ministry of Labour had offered to mediate between employers and workers.

The right of workers to belong to a trade union is safeguarded by Article 19 of the present constitution, but strikes are only permitted provided they are not detrimental to the advancement of the State. The main trade-union organisation is still the Confederation, which is affiliated to the International Confederation of Free Trade Unions and represents the Greek trade-union movement abroad. Its present membership is over 400,000, but the total labour force, excluding civil servants, amounts to some one million persons. More than half of these are members of trade unions which consist either of workers in the same local area or firm, or of workers in the same occupation or industry. Unions in the same local area combine to form labour centres, while unions of workers in the same occupation or industry form nationwide federations.

Employers have their own organisations in the form of associations and federations of associations which are organised on much the same lines, either on a regional basis or by related industries. A special type of professional organisation is the Chamber of Commerce and Industry. Its object is to protect commercial and industrial products, with due consideration for the overall interests of the national economy. These chambers are legal entities and operate in accordance with special laws governing the main urban centres.

WAGES AND PURCHASING POWER

   Price stability and wage and salary increases have had a most favourable effect on workers' real incomes. The upward trend in the minimum wage rates from 1964 onwards has been rapid. In absolute terms the minimum daily wage rate for men increased from £0.890 ($2.133) in 1964 to £1.437 ($3.450) in 1969. The corresponding figures for women were £0.695 ($1.666) and £1.200 ($2.875), respectively. Purchasing power has increased as a result of the stability of the currency and of the general level of prices. Both UN and OECD statistics reveal small increases compared with other countries. In 1969 the consumer price index in Greece increased by 2.48 per cent over 1968 as against 5.48 per cent in the USA, 5.83 per cent in the United Kingdom and 6.10 per cent in France. In terms of real incomes for workers, Greece showed an 18.8 per cent increase between 1968 and 1969. (The increase in both the USA and the United Kingdom was 3.8 per cent.) The real per-capita gross national income rose from £183 ($440) in 1961 to about £229 ($550) in 1966, an annual growth rate of 6.6 per cent. However, it is important to point out that the significance of these average figures is diminished by the considerable existing inequalities in income among regions as well as among groups.

   In terms of their employment many large firms also offer workers a number of fringe benefits, such as cheap meals, holiday camps for children, etc. Under a law of 1958, workers are normally entitled to a family allowance for up to two children, and under special agreements big firms often grant their employees extra family allowances. Salaried personnel are usually paid at half-monthly intervals; wage earners are usually paid on Saturdays.

WOMEN AT WORK

Women have always played a substantial role in the Greek labour force, although this fact is rarely revealed in national statistics. According to the 1961 census only 33.5 per cent of the total female population aged 10 years and over was classified as economically active. Of women in rural areas, only 46.6 per cent declared that they were working to earn a living. These figures do not seem to represent the actual position, especially in the agricultural sector : for most countrywomen the question of survival has always been the most pressing and a far larger percentage perform agricultural work alongside their household duties; with the men they plant, pick, thresh and carry. They are also skilled in weaving, embroidery and rug-making, and the expansion of the tourist industry is now providing wider markets for their work.

Women's participation in industrial work has been gradually increasing since the middle of this century, and is now approaching one-third of the total (rising from 26.8 per cent in 1951 to 32 per cent in 1961). Some decline has occurred in certain fields, such as footwear, chemicals and clothing, and this is attributable to the changing production structure in these groups and the shift to factory production in which women do not participate heavily. Exceptions to this occur in tobacco, textiles, food and beverages, where concentration of production into large-scale factory establishments has favoured the employment of women. They still appear to be the dominant force in footwear, clothing, rubber and paper products.

In the large cities, particularly in Athens, there is a large female population in offices and shops as secretaries and assistants. Unlike the situation in Britain or the United States, however, the catering trade is almost exclusively the domain of men, a reflection of the important role the café and restaurant play in the social life of the Greek male. In principle, there are few restrictions on the employment of women, though they may not be employed on night shifts and in certain hazardous or heavy occupations.

EMIGRATION

Emigration has long had its place in Greek tradition, and throughout this century it has been advanced as one solution to the country's economic problems. Before World War II the United States was the main destination for Greek emigrants; after the war it was replaced by Canada and Australia. A great change in destinations occurred in the early 1960s, when short-range European migration, as opposed to overseas migration, increased at a disturbing rate. Between 1955 and 1957 appeals were made for some thousands of workers for Belgian mines, and since 1960 emigration to West Germany has been organised under a treaty between the Greek Government and the Federal Republic.

In 1962 the number of emigrants (84,918) exceeded the natural increase in population (84,604) and this excess continued during the next three years. From 1966 onwards there was a reduction in the emigration totals, due to the falling off of labour demand in West Germany, and large-scale repatriation of Greek emigrants took place.

In spite of acute psycho-sociological disadvantages at both the local and national levels, emigration has had a compensating effect on the Greek economy. Not only has it lessened the problem of unemployment, it has also greatly strengthened the balance of payments. A Bank of Greece source reveals that total remittances from Greek emigrants increased from £37.5 ($90.5) million in 1960 to £86 ($206.9) million in 1965, with more than half the latter total coming from Western Europe. In Greece, however, the advantages and disadvantages of emigration have to be carefully weighed, and it is true to say that its more favourable aspects have been offset in recent years by its rapid increase.

UNEMPLOYMENT

Although unemployment figures are supplied by labour exchanges, they are imperfect and fail to reflect the picture accurately. According to the censuses of 1951 and 1961, the number unemployed increased from 179,000 to 239,000. In 1961, unemployment was equivalent to 5.5 per cent of the total active working force, while unemployment in the non-agricultural sector was estimated at about 11 per cent. Seasonal unemployment in some agricultural regions has been estimated at between 10 and 25 per cent on an annual basis, and there is also a considerable amount of disguised unemployment in the Greek economy.

There are clear indications, however, that between 1961 and 1966 there was a steady downward trend in unemployment totals and this was due largely to the high rate of emigration. From 1966, when the outflow of emigrants shrank and repatriation began, unemployment was again seen to rise and reach a peak in 1967, when there was wholesale repatriation from West Germany. Data supplied by labour exchanges for 1968 record a figure of 457,592 persons registering for employment, out of which 381,839 were found jobs. At the same time, however, 198,096 persons were discharged by employers.

THE BALANCE OF PAYMENTS

The main characteristic of Greek international trade is the export in large quantities of a few agricultural and mineral products in exchange for a broad spectrum of manufactured goods. Tobacco is the country's most important export commodity, and in 1965 accounted for some 50 per cent of earnings from agricultural exports. In 1969 the Government Committee on Tobacco adopted a new policy designed to lead to a continuous rise in exports and a proportionate increase in production. It is interesting that at present tobacco, in terms of area, rates as a minor crop, occupying under 5 per cent of the cultivated area.

Currants and raisins are the second most important agricultural products, contributing 16 per cent of agricultural export earnings in 1965. Cotton is also one of the more dynamic export commodities and, over the period 1954-64, the value of cotton exports rose by 12 per cent per annum, while its share in agricultural export earnings rose from 8 per cent in 1954 to 13 per cent in 1964. Citrus fruits have increased their share in total agricultural exports from 4 per cent in 1960 to 7 per cent in 1965.

Greece already depends heavily on Common Market countries for sales of certain agricultural items, and in return for free or preferential entry of major farm products to the EEC the country is dismantling its tariffs on EEC goods over periods of twelve to twenty-two years. Important agricultural items from Greece now entering the EEC duty-free are raisins and tobacco. Citrus fruits, olive-oil and wine also receive certain advantages. The Market's agreements with Greece in 1962 evolved from mutual economic incentives rather than any cultural ties and the goal is for eventual customs union, with agricultural and industrial goods flowing freely between the different constituent member countries.

Throughout the 1960s, as previously stated, there was an expansion in the exportation of industrial and handicraft products, amounting to £75 ($177) million in 1969 as against £10 ($25) million in 1965. As a result the ratio of industrial to total exports stood at about 33 per cent, compared with 13 per cent in 1965. The total value of exports in 1969, however, amounted to £162 ($389.3) million, whereas the import bill totalled £482.5 ($1,157.8) million, which was 12.9 per cent higher than in 1968. The trade deficit was closed by the increased earnings from invisible exports, which on balance left a considerable surplus. This emphasises the dependence of the Greek economy on invisible receipts, which are particularly sensitive to changes in political and economic circumstances either at home or abroad. The increase in merchant shipping was mainly due to the expansion of world trade; the increase in emigrants' remittances to the appearance of a labour shortage in Western Europe. Greece cannot in the future expect the same rapid rate of expansion in these revenues. Neither can the country allow its economic development and its foreign exchange needs to become dependent, beyond a certain point, upon the seasonal influx of tourists. Structural weakness in the balance of payments can only be cured by the attainment of a high economic growth rate at the national level.

6

How They Get About

At the conclusion of the civil war the country's communications network was completely disrupted and large capital sums have since been invested in its restoration and further development. The mode of transport, however, can still vary from the unsophistication of a mule to the luxury of the new Aegean helicopter service. In addition to these extremes a well-travelled Greek can be expected to have used caïque, motorbus, steamer, train, private taxi and aeroplane.

The majority of Greeks living on the islands are completely dependent on the wide range of shipping lines that ply from Piraeus and lesser ports. Mainland districts are served by an

---

Away from the main thoroughfares the streets of most Greek towns are unsuitable for modern traffic. The side streets of Salonika present a congested picture of motorcarts, pedestrians and general merchandise.

The bazaar element is equally marked in Athens. In the streets of the old town, shops selling metalwares, bags, carpets and religious ornaments are great attractions for the tourist.

extensive network of local and long-distance buses. The local services are run almost exclusively for the convenience of villagers, taking them to their local market centre in the morning and back in the evening. The 'bone-shaker' bus is still the order of the day, is always overcrowded and usually unpunctual. Service intervals change frequently, often without publicity.

In contrast to the local services the long-distance buses, operated by the joint pools of bus owners (KTEL), maintain accurate schedules in view of the long and often difficult journeys involved. The promoters of these services have strictly interpreted agreements about the places they serve, and their areas of operation are often governed by nome boundaries. The Pullman buses, as they are known in Greece, have high standards of comfort, most of the vehicles being imported from Western European countries. Fares are relatively inexpensive and travelling time is often considerably shorter than by train. The 368-mile journey from Athens to Salonica, for example, is accomplished by Pullman in almost half the time taken by the train.

Salonica is the metropolis of northern Greece and much of the city has been completely modernised since 1950. King Constantine Avenue is lined with tourist offices, fashionable hotels and modern apartment blocks.

The modern gymnasium on the island of Poros reflects something of the improvement in Greek secondary education. The school also serves a number of communities on the Peloponnesian mainland.

H

ROAD

Unlike a number of Western European countries, Greece has no legacy of national highways. The only routeway of historical significance was the Via Egnatia, the large commercial and administrative highway which traversed northern Greece linking Durazzo with Byzantium. East–west communications through the Pindus have always been difficult, and today the mountains are crossed by only two passes: in the north the Metsoven pass leads from Kalabaka to Ioannina; in the south a narrow pass near Mount Timfristos leads from the head-waters of the Sperkhios valley to Karpension.

The major road artery of the country is the national route linking Athens with Salonica via the towns of Lamia, Larisa and Katerini. With the exception of a few sections still being improved, this route approaches almost to motorway standards. In 1969 the Athens-Patras road was inaugurated, forming an extension of the national arterial highway from Athens to Corinth. Traffic counts based on information supplied by the Ministry of Transportation and Public Works (Road Traffic Directorate) illustrate the importance of both these roads, which connect the major cities of Greece with Athens. In 1963 the Corinth Canal road bridge was crossed daily by 1,255 trucks, 424 buses and 1,209 private cars. Similar traffic densities occurred along the Athens-Salonica highway, with the figures naturally increasing near the major urban centres.

In the Peloponnesus, as well as the northern coastal highway which is the axis of the rich agricultural zones of Achaea and Corinth, important routes with heavy traffic-flows serve the fertile plains of Messinia and Laconia. The Peloponnesian road network focuses on the town of Tripolis, sited at the geographical centre of the peninsula. In Thessaly the heaviest traffic occurs in the neighbourhoods of Volos and Larisa, and in northern Greece important roads link Salonica with the principal towns of Macedonia and Thrace.

At the present time a large number of both national and regional roads are either under construction or planned. Work on the biggest road project ever undertaken in Greece concerns the redevelopment of the old Via Egnatia. Ultimately it will join Igoumenitsa, one of the gateways to Greece from Western Europe, with Alexandroupolis near the Turkish frontier. Other important road-development works include the Canea-Iraklion, Thermopyle-Nafpaktos-Antirrion, Salonica-Serrai-Xanthi, and Ioannina-Trikkala highways. During 1968, 620 miles of new road were constructed within the national highway system and maintenance and improvement schemes were carried out over a

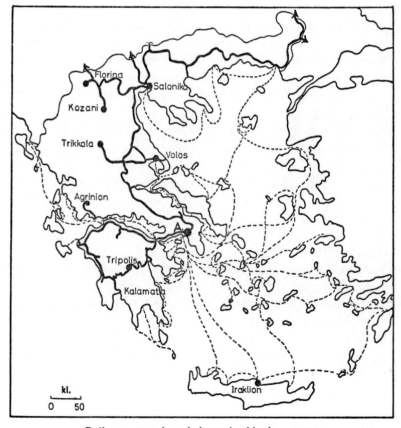

Railway network and domestic shipping routes

total length of 4,960 miles. Within the regional system, 744 miles of new roadway were opened and major repairs and improvements were undertaken on existing roads. There still remain, however, hundreds of communities isolated from the main lines of communication, and it is often easier for a villager to travel to Athens or Salonica than to get to an upcountry community twenty miles away.

RAIL

Greece was one of the last countries in Europe to take up railway development. Consequently the railway network is one of the smallest in Europe and railways play only a small part in the country's transport system. Greece's 1,597 miles of track appear insignificant when compared with the 23,000 miles in operation in France and the 15,000 miles in the United Kingdom. The line linking Athens to Piraeus was constructed in 1867-9, but the main Piraeus-Athens-Larisa line was built only in 1902-9, and did not reach Salonica until 1916. The first international express (Simplon-Orient) ran in July 1920.

Since 1962 Greek railways have been combined into one state enterprise and consist of the former State railroads network (Athens-Northern Greece) of 934 miles, the former network of the Athens-Piraeus-Peloponnesus Railway Company (SPAP), 462 miles, the former Thessalian Railroad Company network (Volos-Kalabaka), 162 miles, and the former North-western Greece Railroad Company (Mesolongi-Agrinion), 39 miles.

The State railroads (SEK) operate on a standard gauge and link Athens and Salonica with the Yugoslav and Turkish frontiers. The remaining networks are of narrow gauge and the largest, the Peloponnesus, connects Athens with the principal centres of southern Greece. In their reconstruction after the civil war no great extension to the railway system was sought once the pre-war level of development was reached.

Greek rail services are generally punctual, but travel tends to be slow and uncomfortable, largely because of the difficult terrain crossed. The famous express trains—the Simplon-Orient, the Tauern, and the Yugoslav-Balkan—which link Greece via Yugoslavia with the principal cities of Western Europe, cover the Athens-Salonica run in an average time of twelve hours. The recently inaugurated Acropolis Express, however, which runs daily between Athens and Munich, has cut the total journey time by eight hours. The introduction of diesel-operated trains in the Peloponnesus and northern Greece has also resulted in speedier schedules.

Most of the existing network is single-track and the inability to integrate this into a uniform-gauge system results in considerable delays in the transportation of goods in Athens from Larisa station (SEK) to Peloponnesus station (SPAP). In 1966 the majority of the locomotives were still steam-driven and approximately half the rolling-stock was more than thirty-five years old. The operation of certain portions of the network is completely uneconomic and the railways as a whole register large annual deficits. In 1964 it amounted to £6 million ($14.5 million).

The transport of goods does not achieve any significant tonnage. In 1961 it was 2,663,000 tons compared with 266 million tons in France. The former State network carries three-quarters of the total tonnage transported, but outside the main Athens-Salonica axis the branch lines are comparatively unimportant. The Athens-Corinth-Patras line has substantial goods traffic, but the remaining Peloponnesus network is of lesser importance, due mainly to the intensive competition from road transport. As an attempt to rejuvenate rail goods traffic a high-speed goods train has been scheduled between Athens and Munich. This will cut travel time from sixty-eight to fifty-seven hours and it is expected to have a decisive effect on the promotion of Greek exports to Western European markets.

The railway problem in Greece has been studied under the sponsorship of the OECD in collaboration with local experts. On the basis of preliminary estimates, railway modernisation and reorganisation will require investments of the order of £50 million ($116 million). In 1968, $8.5 million ($20.3 million) were allocated for improvements, and recent innovations include additional train schedules between Athens-Piraeus and Chalkis, Volos and Orestias on the Turkish frontier. Like goods traffic, passenger-flows on Greek railways also tend to be weak and irregular, again revealing the striking victory of the road. As in the United Kingdom, fare concessions on certain routes during holiday periods and weekends, and fare reductions for excursion parties, are attempts to popularise rail travel and to reduce the deficit margin.

AIR

Greece can be justly proud of its air services, which have made considerable progress in recent years. The country has a number of airports capable of accommodating international air traffic, but the newly completed Athens Central Airport is by far the most important and impressive. This terminal, opened to the public in 1969, is contemporary in style and was inaugurated in time to meet the influx of flight services which have greatly increased recently due to additional flights via Athens by international airlines. At a cost of £13.5 million ($32.6 million) the latest figures have shown a 135 per cent increase in passenger traffic over that of the old terminal.

During the earlier post-war period domestic air services were operated by a State-owned company at a loss. In the mid 1950s Olympic Airways, a private corporation headed by shipping magnate Onassis, was granted exclusive rights to operate within Greece until 1986. As well as linking Athens with major centres in Western Europe, North America and the Middle East, Olympic Airways also operates from Athens a remarkable internal network with daily flights to nineteen provincial centres. A recent innovation is the introduction of a helicopter service to the Saronic and Aegean islands of Spetses, Skiathos, Thera and Myconos, and light-aircraft schedules to Sparta and Porto Heli in the Peloponnesus. This new system of air passenger and goods traffic will have an important influence on tourism in those

Domestic air services

parts of the country inaccessible to conventional aircraft. Domestic air traffic is entirely centred on Athens. There are no provincial points of exchange between the various centres used, although there are some intermediate stops such as Agrinion on the Ioannina line, Larisa and Volos on the Kozani line and Iraklion on the Rhodes line.

The number of passengers served by Olympic Airways was 3,679,000 in 1968, of which 452,199 travelled on overseas flights. The most frequented domestic line is that linking Athens to Salonica which, since 1961, has transported over

100,000 passengers annually at a three-flight daily rate in each direction. The Rhodes line follows with an average since 1961 of 70,000 passengers annually. The vast majority of these are tourists, and in 1968 the company put Boeing 727-200 aircraft into operation on the Athens-Rhodes line to cope with the increased tourist traffic. The lines third in importance serve Crete, and the combined passenger totals for Iraklion and Canea airports average over 100,000 a year.

A rapid rate of activity abroad is also characteristic of Olympic Airways. New overseas flights have recently been inaugurated or extended, including Athens-Nairobi-Johannesburg, Athens-Montreal-Chicago, Rhodes-Nicosia, and a direct London-Rhodes flight. Daily flights by Comet and Boeing aircraft continue to link Athens with Cairo, Tel Aviv, Beirut, Nicosia, Istanbul, Rome, Zurich, Frankfurt, Amsterdam, Paris, London and New York. In total, thirty-seven international companies operate direct air services to Greece.

MERCHANT SHIPPING

From earliest times, shipping has always represented one of the most important branches of the Greek economy, and the maritime traditions of the country were maintained both at the peak of the Byzantine Empire and throughout the Ottoman occupation. Today, a substantial amount of national capital is invested in ocean-going shipping, whilst remittances from shipowners and seamen constitute one of the main revenue items in the balance of payments. In 1969 shipping receipts amounted to £100 million ($243 million), that is, 33.8 per cent of all invisible earnings.

The Greek merchant fleet, badly hit during World War II, by 1958 had more than regained its pre-war strength. Since then it has grown rapidly as revealed in the following figures :

	1958	1969
Number of vessels (Greek flag)	616	2,104
Tonnage (GRT)	1,905	11,139
Number of seamen	14,539	43,500
Transportation exchange ($ million)	60.3	242.1

The merchant fleet under the Greek flag now holds the seventh world place. If ships under Greek ownership but operating under foreign flags are also taken into account, then Greece is numbered amongst the three leading maritime nations of the world, exceeded in gross tonnage only by the United Kingdom and the United States. There are today an estimated 100,000 Greek seamen in employment (56,500 of whom serve on foreign ships), but this available pool is not sufficient to meet the needs of the continuing rapid expansion of the Greek merchant fleet. The establishment of new merchant-marine schools is but one move to meet the current demand.

The primary importance of the shipping industry is that it expresses the cosmopolitan character of the Greek. Through its maritime activities Greece has succeeded in establishing and maintaining close contact with all foreign markets whose trade depends on sea transport. The present government has laid down, and is implementing with strict consistency, an ambitious policy on merchant shipping. The main aims are to increase the role of Greece as a world shipping centre through the repatriation of Greek shipping companies now having offices abroad, and to develop the country's shipbuilding industry along up-to-date and competitive lines. 1969 was christened 'the year of shipping' by the government. Under recent legislation a comprehensive and effective system of incentives has been established to attract foreign shipping offices to Greece. Income-tax relief, customs privileges and the right to duty-free import of household effects, including cars, to their foreign staff meant that by the end of March 1969 126 shipping companies had established their offices in Greece under the provisions of this legislation.

Coastal Shipping

It is not difficult to account for the significance of sea communication in Greece when it is considered that 20 per cent of the country's surface area is taken up by islands supporting a population of around 1.5 million. The domestic steamship service which plies to over 100 small ports is the economic lifeline of these communities and often their only link with the outside world. Piraeus, now one of the largest and busiest international ports in the eastern Mediterranean, is also the Mecca for Greek coastal trade and island communications. The peak months for island travel, due to the tourist influx and Athenian vacations, are July, August and September. A dense network of steamship communications operates between the main island groups, and several small islands, though not accessible by direct regular lines, are linked to the rest by inter-island connections.

The Greek passenger fleet of 314 vessels, ranging from ocean-going liners to small craft with deck accommodation only, is controlled by the Ministry of Mercantile Marine. The Ministry approves and revises sailing schedules with the aim of achieving the best service and avoiding unnecessary simultaneous departures and competition. It also ensures that, during the winter, islands in particular have adequate transport services. Other measures of control concern punctuality, the number of passengers carried and the observance of other safety regulations. Those who have experienced Greek domestic travel to the islands are nonetheless apt to wonder whether much attention is paid to such regulations; intense overcrowding is seldom a reason for not accepting another passenger, and accommodation and food vary greatly from ship to ship—first-class on older boats sometimes falling far below the standard of second-class on newer vessels. Deck accommodation is cheap, and though crowded and uncomfortable it can still be preferable in high summer to sharing a cramped and stuffy cabin in some of the older vessels.

External shipping communications link Greece with all continents. The main port of entry is Piraeus, but there are other points of call for boat services from Western Europe. Regular car ferries operate between Greece and Italy and vessels on the Brindisi-Corfu-Igoumenitsa-Patras run are designed to accommodate 160 passenger cars and 760 persons. Other ferries operate from Venice and Ancona.

PORTS

Until 1870, Ermoupolis (Syra) was the first port of Greece. The opening of the Corinth Canal which attracted shipping between the Adriatic and the Eastern Mediterranean, and the rapid expansion of the Athens conurbation, were the major factors in its decline and the transference of the country's major port activities to Piraeus. Ermoupolis is still an important centre for steamship communications in the Aegean and the island's main revenue comes from maritime trade. Shipbuilding and ship-repairing yards are situated in the southern part of the port, which also serves as a bunkering station mainly to vessels plying to and from the Black Sea.

Modern Piraeus has again become one of the great emporiums of the Levant, a repetition of the situation which existed in classical times when Themistocles constructed the famous Long Walls connecting Athens to its outlet on the Saronic Gulf. The port owes its rebirth to the choice of Athens as capital in 1834, and it is significant that the modern town follows closely the rectangular plan of its ancient predecessor. Piraeus suffered badly during the enemy attacks of World War II, but, now fully restored, it is Greece's greatest industrial and commercial city. It has miles of dockyards, warehouses, factories and industrial plants which combine to give the city its working-class character. It handles 70 per cent of the country's imports, 40 per cent of its exports and 90 per cent of its passenger traffic.

In order to increase the role of Piraeus as an international shipping centre the present government has paid particular attention to the establishment of a complete modern telecommunications system to serve the needs of the large number of Greek and foreign shipping offices. Further developments in the port include the recent agreements with Onassis and Niarchos which will help to turn the whole area between Piraeus and Megara into a huge complex of port and manufacturing installations, approaching in size those of Rotterdam, the world's largest seaport.

Salonica's development as a port is inevitably affected by Greece's relations with her northern neighbour, whose interests are recognised in a Yugoslav free zone. Traditionally Salonica has served as an outlet for the produce of the whole of Macedonia. The recent establishment of industrial zones around the city and heavy investment in its port facilities have resulted in a marked expansion in its trading functions. The present traffic amounts to seven to eight million tons gross cargo, but according to estimates this will increase to fifteen million tons within the next twenty years. Much of this will cover the needs of the adjacent industrial zones in raw materials and exports of manufactured goods.

Patras, Volos and Iraklion are other major ports whose handling facilities have recently been improved and expanded. Patras' manufactures include cotton textiles and motor-tyres, and other products shipped from the port are currants, olive-oil, vallonia, hides and wine. Volos is the main channel of Thessalian exports: cereals, garden produce, cotton, olive-oil, skins, sugar and soap. At one period it rivalled the industrial potential of Piraeus until stricken by the disastrous earthquakes of 1954 and 1955. The central position of Iraklion and its good communications with the mainland makes this city the major port for Crete. Developments in a host of smaller ports throughout Greece have been geared mainly to the expanding tourist industry.

TRAFFIC PROBLEMS

Traffic congestion, which for long has occupied first place in the thoughts of western planners, is now an acute worry to Greece, or at least to Athens, which suffers from imminent traffic paralysis. In 1968 Greece spent a total of £29.5 million ($71 million) on the import of motor vehicles, tyres and spare parts. Expenditure has increased from year to year almost without a break and in 1968 accounted for 6.1 per cent of total imports. The continuous rise in private incomes and the growth of domestic passenger and goods traffic has led to an increase in the demand for cars and motorcycles, which is met almost wholly by imports. Greece has no integrated motor industry and manufacturing is confined to the production of a few types of bodies, mainly for buses, and to tyres.

The sharp rise in the number of motor vehicles in circulation began in 1953, when restrictions were lifted on almost all imports, including cars. Between 1954 and 1968 motor vehicles in circulation increased almost sevenfold :

Motor Vehicles in Circulation (in thousands)

	1954	1967	1968
Passenger cars	15.1	145.5	169.1
Buses	5.4	9.5	9.7
Lorries	18.8	81.2	87.1
Motorcycles	7.6	58.4	62.6
	46.9	294.6	328.5

The greatest rise was in the number of passenger cars, which increased elevenfold, despite the fact that import duty, levies and other charges make the purchase of a car expensive for the Greek buyer. Furthermore there were eight times as many motorcycles in 1968 as in 1954 and nearly five times as many lorries. The lowest rise was in the number of buses, in which the increase was almost twofold.

Despite this increase the ratio of total motor vehicles to population is still low compared to western countries. According to the figures for the end of 1968 there were 37 vehicles (including motorcycles) per thousand inhabitants, or one vehicle for every 27 inhabitants. The figure for passenger cars was 19 per thousand persons as compared with 334 in us, 212 in France, 187 in Britain, 171 in Germany and 141 in Italy. The problem in Greece, however, is that three-quarters of the total motor vehicles are concentrated in and around the capital area.

Great importance is now being attached to solving the Athens traffic problem. Among the more original measures being considered is the construction of an underground rail system based on a study by French communication experts. The existing Piraeus-Athens-Kifissia electric railway, which is partly underground, consists of one route only, and although trains are frequent congestion is acute. The high density of buses and trams that serve the capital from about 5.30am to midnight adds greatly to traffic congestion. The new Athens bus terminus, serving both urban and inter-urban lines, was planned on the basis of relieving congestion in a large part of the city.

7

How They Learn

EDUCATION, no less than other aspects of national life, has suffered adversely from Greece's turbulent history. Oppression, revolution and war have created serious difficulties and done little to foster creative intellect. Prior to Greek independence, education and religion were firmly interwoven and village priests acted as local teachers to the children of their parishes. In 1833 education was brought within a State system which remained largely unaltered until 1928. Attendance at primary school was made compulsory for all children of six years of age and this could be followed by a secondary education which was neither compulsory nor free. Teachers' training colleges were also early established, together with the Athens Polytechnic (1836) and University (1837).

The early education framework remained an ideal rather than a reality owing to great practical difficulties. Progress was hindered by the country's poverty. School buildings were inadequate, teachers were too few, their salaries a mere pittance, and in spite of the law many children failed to attend school. Political unrest and the absence of a permanent civil service also created serious problems. Large-scale dismissals or transfers of teachers to remote villages if their political leanings, however mild, offended the government of the day, were common.

The language question also complicated educational development, perhaps more so than any other single factor. Closely linked with party politics, the question as to whether the demotic or *katharevousa* tongue should be taught in schools virtually meant that with every change in government there

133

was a change in the medium of education. The language conflict has continued to the present time, and the present government, as part of its educational 'reforms', reverted to the custom of teaching children above the third class of elementary school *katharevousa* Greek. It is not surprising that the education system this century has borne the imprint of confusion! During his years of compulsory primary education the Greek child often learns a different grammar and a different spelling from those he is taught afterwards in the more advanced stages of schooling.

Compared with the early decades of this century, however, Greek education has considerably improved, especially from 1950 onwards. Graduates of higher educational institutions as a percentage of the total population aged thirteen years and over increased from 1.6 per cent in 1951 to 2.0 per cent in 1961. The corresponding percentage of high-school and elementary-school graduates also increased, respectively, from 5.5 per cent and 29.5 per cent in 1951 to 8.0 per cent and 45.2 per cent in 1961. The proportions of those not graduating from elementary school and of illiterates declined, respectively, from 63.2 per cent and 25.8 per cent in 1951 to 44.8 per cent and 18.8 per cent in 1961. Since 1961 the educational level of the Greek population

---

The Saronic island of Hydra is a popular vacation centre for Athenians and continental tourists. It is also an established centre for artists, attracted by the unique character of its town and landscape.

Myconos rivals Hydra in its popularity. Cubic houses of rough stone, plastered over and then whitewashed, are characteristic of the Cyclaves Islands.

has continued to improve, but it still remains low in comparison with corresponding levels in Western Europe. For example, in Italy high-school and university graduates reached 17.7 per cent of the total employed labour force in 1961, compared with 10.7 per cent in Greece, while in other Western European countries the comparison is even more unfavourable for Greece. In general, lack of funds, outmoded buildings, a shortage of teachers and the existence of a parochial attitude towards change present great problems to progress. Under Papandreou a positive policy of modernisation was inaugurated. Compulsory schooling was extended from six to nine years and free meals in all elementary schools in the countryside, with a limited number of scholarships to secondary schools, made the new provisions realistic in a country where poor parents would rather use their children's labour. Corporal punishment was officially banned from all Greek schools, and to meet the desperate shortage of teachers their period of training was reduced from three to two years. Free school meals and the extension of the school-leaving age were both abolished by the colonels directly after the 1967 *coup*, and this again serves to illustrate the effect of governmental change and political instability on the continuity of educational programmes.

———

An extensive bus network serves the mainland but most journeys are slow and uncomfortable. The scene at one of Iraklion's bus stations is repeated throughout the country.

From Myconos motorboats leave daily, transporting holiday-makers to the main island beaches. A regular service by caïque to the archaeological ruins of Delos is also conducted from the island.

I

Had the law raising the school-leaving age from twelve to fifteen remained, this would certainly have been difficult to enforce. Owing to the shortage of teaching staff, political up-heavals and the problems of supervising the remote and less prosperous districts, Greece has always had a high proportion of its population above the age of twelve which has failed to complete an elementary school course. In 1961 it amounted to 44.8 per cent of the total population but varied regionally from 28.7 per cent in Greater Athens to 61.8 per cent in Thrace.

It is not surprising, therefore, that the 1961 census revealed an illiteracy rate of 18.8 per cent of the adult population. On a regional basis illiteracy varied from 10 per cent of the adult population in Greater Athens to 22 per cent, 25 per cent and 30 per cent in Epirus, the Ionian Islands and Thrace, respectively. 70.2 per cent of illiterates, however, belonged to the age groups of forty-five and above, and there was a marked discrepancy between male illiteracy (8 per cent) and female illiteracy (27 per cent).

Contemporary governments have been fully aware of the close interdependence between education and economic growth, and large capital sums have been invested in education pro-grammes. In an attempt to increase the output of technical and scientific graduates a number of government-run technical schools were initiated under the education reforms of 1959 and 1963-5. Yet science graduates still represent only 25 per cent of all graduates from higher education, as compared with 50 per cent in the EEC. In 1968 the present government inaugurated a crash programme for the modernisation of all grades of education. It was accompanied by a 'purge' of the teaching profession which, like the civil service in general, was largely inefficient. It is known, however, that schools and colleges were also purged of all teachers of reformist and creative bent and particularly those with anti-government affiliations. Around 150 senior university teachers have been dismissed in the past three years, a number of them being the country's leading scientists and scholars. An important innovation has been the free issue of basic textbooks to pupils and students, and since 1968 these have totalled over 26,000,000. To see this development in its true light, however, it must also be stated that a forty-page list of banned books has been circulated and textbooks have been rewritten in the light of the aims of the April revolution.

Governmental control is naturally strongest at university level, where chancellors and vice-chancellors are now appointed by the minister and not, as formerly, by university senates. Candidates for university are scrutinised by the security police, a special branch of which is organised to observe students. It is extremely difficult to appraise the impact of current government policy on Greek education, but one thing is certain : education is irrevocably bound up with liberty, a right denied to Greek students and teachers today. If education is to aid economic growth, freedom of expression for the fruitful transmission of ideas is a prerequisite. Dictatorial control will serve only to wreck further an academic life which showed signs of a great awakening in the early sixties.

ELEMENTARY EDUCATION

Since 1961 there has been a substantial increase in the number of infants entering kindergartens. In 1967 they totalled 52,253, compared with around 34,000 in 1961. Attendance is not compulsory, and children between the ages of three-and-a-half and five-and-a-half are given a two-year preparatory period for going to elementary school. The upward trend in numbers is a reflection of the increasing urbanisation of the Greek population, the general improvement in urban standards of living and the increased participation of women in productive work.

Education for most Greek children begins with entry to the elementary school at the age of five-and-a-half to six. In the State-controlled schools education is free, but Greece also has a large number of fee-paying private schools, and education owes much to the generous endowment of institutions both by wealthy Greeks and foreigners. In 1967 there were 10,294 schools providing elementary education, of which 9,647 were State-administered and 647 privately administered. These had a teaching staff of 27,979 and a total of 975,839 pupils. There is, however, a 16 per cent drop-out of pupils who do not continue their education to the legal school-leaving age of twelve.

The teacher, who is someone of authority, especially in rural areas, covers the standard academic curriculum—reading, writing, arithmetic, geography, history (with the emphasis on the ancient and modern history of Greece), and the Greek language, as well as some religion. Schools are controlled and supervised by the Ministry of Education, which also prescribes the curriculum. Teaching methods vary considerably, but the traditional method of rote learning is very common.

Although notable progress has been achieved in elementary education, the condition of school buildings and equipment and the general standard of teaching are still far from satisfactory. A survey undertaken in 1962 revealed that school equipment was rudimentary to the extent that 50 per cent of elementary schools were inadequately provided with such bare necessities as benches and blackboards. Library facilities and gymnastic and games equipment were also poor. Since 1962 over 6,000 schools have been equipped with laboratory facilities for teaching scientific subjects such as physics and chemistry.

An acute shortage of teachers has been a major factor in the unsatisfactory functioning of elementary education. In 1967, 42 per cent of the schools were one-teacher establishments and only 12 per cent had the full contingent of six teachers. In this connection Greece faces problems common to other countries in that teachers are reluctant to accept positions in small and isolated communities. In many villages, especially in Northern Greece, the local priest is forced to serve as the primary school teacher, reverting to the practice common under Turkish rule. Of the present total of elementary teachers 45 per cent are women and the present pupil-to-teacher ratio is 35 : 1 as compared with 40 : 1 in 1960-1. This, however, is a national average and fails to draw attention to the significant differences between educational districts and between schools in the same district. Most elementary classes are overcrowded and in Athens the pupil-to-teacher ratio varies between 45 and 50:1.

SECONDARY EDUCATION

Secondary education admits pupils from elementary schools after an entry examination and its divided into two cycles, each lasting three years. The raising of the school-leaving age to fifteen would mean that all children would experience a period of at least three years at the gymnasium. Secondary education is widely regarded as an important source of family pride as well as a sound investment but many Greek children find it extremely difficult, if not impossible, to attend a gymnasium. They are found only in sizeable settlements and this frequently causes great expense and difficulty for the child in attendance. In the islands, for example, only the most affluent families find it possible to send their children to gymnasiums.

Formerly the first cycle of a gymnasium course consisted of an arduous three-year period of study which included ancient and modern Greek, Latin and French. Little attention was given to scientific subjects, with the result that, on finishing secondary school, the intellectual equipment of the pupil was pretty lightweight. The second cycle covered a further three years, where again a strong emphasis was placed on the humanities. Today the gymnasiums offer a wider range of subjects, particularly in the sciences, and the senior cycle is divided into a theoretical and practical section. In the former the emphasis is on the humanities and in the latter priority is given to the study of applied sciences. It is possible to transfer from one section to the other.

In 1967 around 430,000 pupils attended State-administered and private gymnasiums. Of this total 22,479 attended night schools run for children engaged in earning a living during the day. A serious problem facing secondary education is the high proportion of drop-outs, which reaches 50 per cent of the intake in certain years. Other problems concern buildings and equipment, which are far from satisfactory. The 1962 survey drew attention to intense overcrowding and the absence in many schools of basic facilities such as piped water, electric light and adequate sanitation. Moreover there was a desperate need for some 93,000 desks and 2,700 blackboards as well as other basic items. The quality of education varies considerably from area to area and school to school, and here it should be pointed out that a number of the privately administered schools are of a particularly high standard. Many are run on American and British public school lines and they have done much for the secondary education of girls in particular. Private schools are normally beyond the reach of the average Greek child because of their high fees. The examination taken at the end of a secondary school career acts as a qualification for entry into higher educational institutions.

SCHOOL HEALTH AND WELFARE

Greece has recently been taking the problems of school health and welfare most seriously. The task of supervising pupils attending elementary and secondary school belongs to the school health division of the Ministry of Education. In addition to the general health inspectors in Athens and Salonica there are 24 school health sanitary inspectors, 174 school doctors, 32 school nurses and 26 school health centres for the medical examination of pupils. The supervision of school buildings so that they conform to basic hygienic conditions also falls to the school health division. Since 1929 school doctors have given systematic teaching on hygienic principles, the latter being an obligatory subject in secondary school classes. Female pupils are also given advice and instruction on infant care and related problems. An average of 20,000 pupils are medically examined each year in school health centres.

Within the last few years physical education has received a great deal of government assistance. Larger credits have been allocated to complete installations, to improve existing facilities and to build new physical recreation centres for all grades of education. As part of the school welfare programme an average of 45,000 children and working adolescents spend their summer vacations in youth camps run by the Ministry of Social Services. In addition, there are camping sites for school children run by private organisations, insurance firms and municipalities, as well as camps owned by the Ministry of Education. In order to develop further the artistic and cultural interests of school children various bodies annually hold exhibitions of paintings and craftwork and promote plays, concerts and literary festivals. The Boy Scout and Red Cross organisations actively encourage the exchange of ideas through school pen clubs and cultural tours abroad.

TECHNICAL AND VOCATIONAL TRAINING

Technical and vocational training in Greece falls under the auspices of a number of authorities including the Ministries of Labour, Agriculture, Social Welfare and Education, and the Merchant Marine. The founding of new technical institutions in provincial areas has greatly aided the decentralisation of this branch of education and the share of the Athens area in the total number of technical students declined from 60 per cent in 1961 to 50 per cent in 1967.

Technical education is conducted at lower, intermediate and higher grades. Courses in the lower grade begin at the age of twelve and generally last for three years. In the intermediate and higher grades a four-year course is common, with practical training included in this period. On the lower and intermediate levels a total of 457 public and private institutions functioned during 1965-6, with a teaching staff of 6,348 and a student population of 81,244. Technical and vocational training is now the subject of a comprehensive development programme geared to the country's economic needs, and institutions of manufacturing, engineering, construction, tourism and wholesale and retail trade are increasing. There are also a number of specialised agricultural schools concerned with modern farming methods and their practical application to the Greek environment. The American Farm School in Salonica trains personnel in scientific farming techniques and also carries out extensive research into the problems of Greek agriculture.

Greece has a number of special schools for the training of nurses and the promotion of this profession has received much encouragement in recent years. Other forms of vocational education include the training of merchant marine officers, preparatory schools for careers in the army, navy and air force, training for administrative posts in the civil service, religious seminaries and social welfare schools. There has also been an increase in the number of institutions offering training for teachers.

THE UNIVERSITIES

Until recently there were only two universities in Greece, one in Athens and the other in Salonica. Of equivalent status, however, are the National Polytechnic, the Graduate School of Economics and Commercial Science, the School of Fine Arts, the Panteios Graduate School of Political Science, and industrial and agricultural graduate colleges in Athens, Piraeus and Salonica. The overwhelming concentration of higher-education institutions in Athens and Salonica was one of the reasons which led to the development of the University of Patras, opened in 1968, and the University of Ioannina, which is under construction. There has also been serious discussion over a university for Crete and for Thessaly at Larisa. The number of students at university level increased from 35,432 for the 1962-3 academic year to 64,591 in 1966-7. The teaching staff, although still inadequate for the number of students, increased from 1,066 to 2,541.

The University of Athens was founded as a State university in 1837 and incorporated the Ionian Academy, an institution established by Lord Guilford in 1824 as a centre of university education in the Ionian Islands. Athens University quickly developed as an important education centre for the Greek world, though its early history was a troubled one, with student demonstations against authority appearing decades ahead of their time. The university, like many other Greek institutions, benefited substantially from the generosity of wealthy benefactors, in this case Domboli, who left funds in 1854 which were to accumulate for fifty-seven years and then to be used to endow a university in memory of Capodistrias. Capodistrias had been elected Governor of Greece in 1827 and in memory of his achievements the University of Athens changed its name in 1911 to the National and Capodistrian University. It was divided for financial, though not for academic purposes, into two parts, one receiving a subsidy from the State, the other living off the income from the Domboli bequest.

In 1965 Athens University had a student population of nearly 17,000 and a lecturing staff of 657. It offers mainly advanced courses in science, letters, law, theology and medicine, preparing students for professional practice. The students take intermediate examinations on each year's curriculum, their registration for the next year being dependent upon success in these examinations. Students who have completed the required period of attendance and succesfully passed all intermediate examinations can be permitted to sit the graduate examinations. Entry competition to all Greek universities is tough, and overcrowding, with low academic and recreational facilities, is common. The site of the University City of Athens has finally been settled and plans are in progress for its construction.

The Aristotelian University in Salonica is a larger institution, having in 1965 nearly 20,000 students and a teaching staff of 800. It has always been regarded as more progressive than Athens and was founded in 1925 to meet the increasing needs of the country and especially those of the northern provinces. From the time of its foundation the emphasis has been on the more practical and technical aspects of the studies taught, together with the study of Balkan problems. Thus schools of agriculture, forestry, veterinary medicine and Balkan history were established alongside philosophy, natural sciences, mathematics and law etc. Like Athens it is an autonomous institution governed by a senate of professors and supported by and under the general supervision of the State.

The National Polytechnic of Athens is an old institution whose foundation pre-dates that of Athens University by one year. There have, however, been considerable breaks in its history and re-establishments took place in 1887 and 1914. The Polytechnic has adequately equipped laboratories and workshops and offers technical instruction in a wide variety of disciplines. Like the institutions mentioned above, it has university status but is incapable of servicing the great demand for scientific education. Many Greeks are forced to study at universities abroad to gain qualifications in scientific and technical subjects.

The recent large increase in the number of students at university level has not been accompanied by a corresponding increase in teaching personnel, university buildings and general amenities. Thus the average overall student-teacher ratio, which in 1961-2 was 31 : 1, worsened considerably, reaching 41 : 1 in 1964-5. In 1961 the ratio was 17 : 1 in England and Wales, 14 : 1 in Austria, 12 : 1 in Spain and 9 : 1 in Italy. The standard of teaching also leaves much to be desired. Lectures are few and academically stilted, tutorials are uncommon and the student receives little of the guided instruction he would expect in Britain and the United States. The absence of organised postgraduate study in Greek universities and the low level of university research is a reflection of the unsatisfactory nature of undergraduate training. The student, too, faces financial difficulties. Textbooks are in short supply and since most of them, particularly for scientific and technical subjects, are published abroad, they are expensive. Scholarships to Greek universities are available and the granting of loans to students has been approved. Unlike Britain, these loans have to be repaid in instalments commencing two years after the conclusion of the student's course. For financial reasons many Greek students are forced to take part-time jobs and it is not uncommon for young men to work exceptionally long hours for a number of years in order to save enough money to support a period of university training abroad. It is significant that 59 per cent of Greek students at universities abroad study scientific and technical subjects.

In order to improve the distribution of students between arts and science subjects, it is planned to orientate the new universities towards sciences and applied science in general. Special emphasis is also being given to organising post-graduate scientific education. The lack of post-graduate opportunities, to date, has forced a large number of young scientists to study and research at foreign universities. Particular emphasis is now being laid on the provision of adequate laboratories and equipment in order to attract the appropriate scientific personnel.

In conclusion, education is a vital factor in the social and cultural development of Greece. The improvement in the level of education and the skill of the labour force is also a basic requirement for achieving the planned high rate of productivity and a main prerequisite for the long-term development of the economy. Besides the planned educational reforms Greece has also aimed at creating opportunities for education outside the formal system and particularly in rural areas. Much discussion has centred around the expansion of educational radio programmes and the development of a television coverage with educational programmes for the greater part of the country. Every encouragement and financial support is being given to local government organisations and other foundations that show initiative in developing educational and cultural activities in provincial areas.

8

How They Amuse Themselves

THE Greeks often find it difficult to differentiate work from leisure. Their great attachment to life in general and their inexhaustible imagination liberate their spirits from the confines of a dull workaday world. The low standard of living which has characterised the country this century has taught the Greeks the secret of amusing themselves with little or no money, and their aptitude for improvisation has developed for Greece a type of entertainment wholly typical and peculiar to its people.

In spite of the fact that private expenditure on organised leisure activities has increased rapidly since 1960, it averaged only £4.15 ($10) per head of population in 1967, although wide differences existed throughout the country, especially between rural and urban areas. Even in Athens, however, the average Greek has undemanding tastes and derives extreme pleasure from the simple things of life.

A great deal of leisure time, especially in summer, is spent outside the house, and this is as much a reflection of the Greek's love of crowds and conversation and his abhorrence of solitude as of an ideal climate for open-air relaxation. As in ancient times the house appears little more than a place in which to sleep, and social life is conducted in the streets, the squares and, above all, in the cafés. The café is where the heart is and the focal point of leisure activities. Cafés fall into a number of types of establishment but it is the *kafeneion* or coffee house which plays a major role in Greek social life. This is an austere establishment usually thronged with male patrons for whom it is both local club and

148

political forum. A stranger to Greece may conclude that the clientele of the *kafeneion* is composed of people who have nothing better to do than to sit there interminably. This would be a mistake, as much business is transacted in the coffee house, appointments are made and kept, and the latest news, political and commercial, is exchanged and discussed. In rural Greece the coffee house is the key social institution of the village where inhabitants meet to discuss agricultural problems and community affairs. Whether in town or village the coffee house is where public opinion is formed, and it is here that local and national politicians must win their battles. Indeed, during elections, the coffee houses are the arenas where candidates for political office deliver their speeches and vie for votes.

Catering establishments in Greece are crowded at all times of the day, but it is during late evening that they reach their peak of activity. In many districts of Athens they remain open all night and are crowded until the early hours of the morning. It is indicative of the Greek's simple tastes that in spite of a rising standard of living and an annual increase in organised entertainment in Athens, which is related to the upsurge in tourist activity, the average Athenian prefers to sit and watch the world go by at a pavement café.

An interesting survey was undertaken in the mid-1960s by the Athens Centre of Ekistics. It concerned the participation of Athenians in community recreation facilities. Eighteen sample areas were studied and these were arranged into five groups on the basis of average per-capita incomes. The communities ranged from very-high-income areas such as Kolonaki and Kefalari which averaged over 3,300drs a month, through high, medium, low to very-low-income areas such as Petropoulis and Koukouvaones with below 650drs a month. A general idea of the intensity with which certain facilities were used by the population of the eighteen communities is shown in the following table and was computed for men, women and young people (eighteen years of age and under).

*Percentage who used facility at least once
in week (or month) preceding survey*

	Men	Women	Young People
Coffee houses	29.3	0.7	0.7
Confectioners	25.0	22.5	18.0
Tavernas	13.9	7.7	2.4
Restaurants	7.0	2.8	1.0
Night clubs	1.6	1.1	0.4
Cinemas	42.3	41.0	37.4
Theatres	10.1	9.6	3.8
Gymnasiums	0.6	0.2	2.2
Football games	5.4	0.2	3.0
Other athletic events	1.8	0.2	1.9
Parks	6.7	9.3	12.2

The survey substantiated the fact that visiting coffee houses is almost exclusively a male pastime. In the poorest communities, coffee houses were frequented by 34.1 per cent men and 0.2 per cent women, and in the wealthiest communities by 12.3 per cent men and 2.3 per cent women. Visits to confectioners showed little discrimination on the basis of sex, but there was an important social discrimination in that the confectioners rather than coffee houses were favoured by the higher-income groups. The predominantly male use of *tavernas* and restaurants was also marked, but for the population as a whole Athenians show a somewhat greater propensity to dine out than is common in Britain or the United States. The distinction between a restaurant proper and a *taverna* is not clearly definable, but in general the latter is less formal, is patronised for a convivial evening rather than for luncheon, and its fare is usually uncompromisingly Greek.

Throughout the summer months the nightly exodus of Athenians leads them to the surrounding suburbs and particularly to the Saronic coast with its wealth of restaurants, *tavernas* and bars. Within the city itself the night entertainment centre is the Plaka, the old town at the foot of the Acropolis. This is a favourrite haunt of Athenians and tourists alike, but the popularity of the district has tended to inflate prices at its countless eating-houses and small night clubs. Many of the new forms of organised entertainment in Athens and elsewhere are western-inspired and are geared to the annual influx of tourists. This is particularly true of the islands of Myconos, Hydra, Rhodes and Corfu, where night clubs and discotheques have produced a cosmopolitan atmosphere similar to the tourist coasts of the western Mediterranean. The Saronic coast and the Aegean Islands are popular vacation areas for Athenians. During summer weekends and throughout the month of August all available accommodation is taken and the policy of renting or building a summer house in vacation areas has increased rapidly in recent years.

FEASTS AND FESTIVALS

The Greeks observe a great number of religious feast days which play an important part in the life of the country, sometimes to the detriment of productivity. Until recently Greek civil servants took twenty-five religious days' holiday every year. The Christian legacy of the country has been shaped from deeply rooted traditions and ancient rites, with the result that a large number of superstitious and pagan customs accompany the pomp and circumstance of the Byzantine ritual. The various powers and characteristics of the ancient gods and demigods of mythology have become embodied in Christian saints and many ancient beliefs, under the guise of religious ceremonial, strongly colour religious festivals, in rural areas in particular.

Most religious ceremonies coincide with those of western Christendom since the adoption of the Gregorian calendar in 1923. Exceptions are Easter and Whitsun, which are still based on the Julian style and occur, therefore, anything up to a month later. Easter has by far the most important religious ceremonies, and in Athens they are performed with great pomp and are attended by the heads of state. Universal mourning reaches a climax in the evening of Good Friday when every parish church holds a funeral procession, the flower-covered symbolical bier followed by the clergy and the highest dignitaries. At the midnight service on Saturday the period of mourning ends and Easter Sunday is given over to popular rejoicing with lambs roasting on the spit and folk-dancing. Easter coincides, at least as regards the season, with the great spring festivities of antiquity, which were meant to celebrate the awakening of nature after the winter months. Christmas is now more widely celebrated, and decorations, carols and Christmas trees are common in Athens.

Throughout Greece 15 August is a specially important religious feast day, being that of the Dormition of the Virgin Mary which is equivalent to the Assumption of the Virgin in other lands. As saints' days are more important than birthdays in Greece, even for young children, 15 August is an important name day for the countless Marys. A large proportion of Greek Christian names are derived from saints and a name day is celebrated with family reunions. Saints Constantine and Helen are celebrated on 21 May and traditionally this marks the beginning of summer, when indoor cinemas and theatres close and outdoor life begins.

Religious feast days are of great significance to the local community. Every village keeps its own festival on the day of its patron saint, generally the saint to whom the church is dedicated. Impressive services and popular fairs are common. On 25 March and 15 August thousands of pilgrims, devout and otherwise, converge on the Panaghia Evanghelistria Church on the Cycladic island of Tinos. This church, in effect, is the Lourdes of Greece and miracles are reputed from an icon discovered in Tinos in 1822. A large number of sick and maimed increase the population on these special days. In the Macedonian villages of Langadas and Aghia Heleni, 21 May is celebrated by the festival of the *Anastenarides* or Firewalkers. Numerous visitors, including men of science and students of anthropolgy, flock to these villages to witness the strange ritual whose pagan origins are lost in antiquity. The adherents to the cult, after many hours of rhythmic dancing, start treading a blazing bed of charcoal embers and seem to come to little harm. Salonica celebrates its patron saint in a less frenzied manner. Here during the month of October the memory of Saint Demetrius is evoked in the

Demetria, a festival which aims at reviving the Byzantine traditions of the city through a series of religious and artistic events.
Not all festival days are religious. 25 March is also Independence Day, which remembers the long struggle for independence
from the Turkish occupation. This day of nationwide commem-
oration is celebrated annually with great national feeling and
military parades are held at the two principal cities, Athens and
Salonica. The anniversary of the rejection of Mussolini's ultima-
tum to Greece during World War II is on 28 October and is the
second of the two principal national holidays. It is known as
Ochi Day, the Greek word for 'no'. The carnival period depends
on the date fixed for Easter and begins for a period of three
weeks ten Sundays before Easter Sunday. It gives rise to colourful
manifestations all over the country, but especially in Patras, in
the Plaka district of Athens, Corfu and Zante. Accompanying
all festivals, religious and national, and also marriages, births
and baptisms, are the traditional Greek dances and songs whose
fundamental lines and texts have remained little altered for
centuries.

A number of other festivals occur in Greece which are neither
religious nor national but are principally aimed at the country's
tourist market. Many of them, like the *Demetria* in Salonica, are
cultural. The highlight is, no doubt, the Athens Festival, firmly
established as one of the world's outstanding artistic events.
In concept it is not unlike the the Edinburgh Festival, and internationally renowned conductors, soloists, orchestras and theatre
companies present concerts, operas, classical and modern plays
in the superb frame of the ancient theatre of Herodes Atticus
at the foot of the Acropolis. It is sponsored for the summer
months by the National Tourist Organisation, and since its
inauguration in 1955 it has rapidly developed into a major
artistic event.

RADIO AND TELEVISION

The National Broadcasting Institution has been a State
K

supervised organisation since 1939. It offers a choice of three programmes, National, Second and Third, broadcast from trans-
mitters situated on the outskirts of Athens. The National
Programme presents informative, cultural and light entertainment
items, the Second Programme entertainment only, and the Third
Programme broadcasts serious music for five hours a day with
a short five-minute news bulletin in English, French and German.
There is in addition a short-wave station broadcasting programmes directed to foreign listeners. The NBI is financed by
licence fees, government grants and revenue derived from commercial advertising on the Second Programme.

The Greeks like the radio, especially the Second Programme,
which blares out incessantly in cafés, buses and shops. The
number of radio receivers, however, is not particularly high,
and this may help to explain why the Greek is willing to share
his favourite programme with his less fortunate compatriots. In
1965 there were 99 radio receivers for every 1,000 inhabitants,
compared with 294 in the United Kingdom.

Television is still in the experimental stage and programme
coverage is limited. It is very much dependent on British and
American programmes which are specially sub-titled for national
transmission. In view of the recent arrival of television in Greece
it is too early to judge the impact it will have on leisure activities.
Within the past few years over 100,000 television sets have
been installed in Athenian homes, which seems to suggest that
the public interest is substantial. Price, however, puts television
out of the reach of the majority of Greeks, but the government
has been active in its efforts to install TV units in public buildings
of villages of less than 1,000 inhabitants.

CINEMA

Cinema-going in Greece is an extremely popular pastime and
over 2,500 enclosed and open-air cinemas existed in 1967. The
Ekistics Survey revealed that for Athens the average weekly
attendance was 42.3 per cent men, 41.0 per cent women and

37.4 per cent young people. Weekly attendance is therefore considerably higher than in Britain and the United States, and this demand is reflected in the frequency with which general-release cinemas change their programmes. Cinemas exist even in the smallest settlements and in Athens the suburban cinema is one of the first facilities to appear amidst multi-storeyed housing blocks. First-run cinemas, which formerly were almost exclusively confined to the central area of the city, have also invaded the suburbs, particularly the better-class residential areas. The reason for this is largely related to the fact that cinema-going is most popular among the middle income communities who demand and get the best of American, British, French and German films.

In spite of the general popularity of the cinema, the Greek film-making industry is poorly organised and specialises to a large extent in cheaply and badly produced films for provincial audiences. Some eighty films are produced annually and are mainly emotional dramas and unsubtle comedies which appeal to Greek humour. By far the majority of films shown in Athens and the provinces, however, are dubbed or subtitled foreign films. From time to time Greek films win international acclaim, an example being *Never on Sunday,* but these are specially produced for foreign audiences and are in no way comparable with the domestic varieties.

One film producer who has acquired international recognition in recent years is Michael Cacoyannis whose films are deeply rooted in the Greek life and landscape. His important films have included *Windfall in Athens* (1954), *Stella* (1955), *The Girl in Black* (1956) and *A Matter of Dignity* (1957). Although they have been challenged by some critics as being undisciplined in script and uneven in direction, Cacoyannis has a strong feeling for atmosphere. His highly successful *Zorba the Greek* was produced for international release.

The effect which television will have on cinema audiences remains to be seen. The spectacular drop of cinema attendances in Britain when television became popular might well be repeated in Greece. Yet the importance of outdoor life, including attendance at the open-air cinema, should combat the appeal of television, especially during the summer months.

THEATRE

Theatrical life is naturally concentrated in Athens, where there are some twenty-four winter and twelve summer theatres, the latter specialising in light musical comedies of local appeal. Salonica, Patras and Rhodes possess good theatres, and smaller ones are to be found in other towns, but in general theatrical life in the provinces is on a limited scale. The commercial theatre, consisting of private companies, receives State support in the form of interest-free loans which can amount to £50,000 ($120,000) for each company in each theatrical season. These are repaid from a percentage of the company's takings. In Athens the National Theatre and the National Opera Company, and in Salonica the North of Greece State Theatre, are financed directly by the state.

The National Theatre was founded in 1900 but early in its career it ran into financial difficulties and was forced to close down in 1908. It was re-established under State auspices in 1930 and after the complete renovation of the Royal Theatre its first performances were given in March 1932. From the very beginning the National Theatre has been deeply preoccupied with the revival of ancient drama, and from 1936 onwards it became more and more convinced that it should be played in natural surroundings in the open air. It was not until 1954, however, that the ancient theatre of Epidaurus was used for productions, and following its immediate success and popular appeal a regular annual festival has been held there ever since, under the control of the National Tourist Organisation. In summer the National Theatre also plays at the Odeum of Herodes Atticus and at the ancient theatres of Delphi and Dodoni.

Presenting ancient Greek drama for modern audiences has its problems and the National Theatre has undertaken much searching experimentation and calculation in choosing its broad

lines of interpretation. It is realised that the museum-piece presentation is an artistic cul-de-sac, and that the essential dramatic
and poetic elements must be projected in a manner that is mean-
ingful to the present-day audience. The tours of the National
Theatre, especially from the 1950s onwards, have guaranteed
it an international audience and a high reputation abroad.
Within Greece itself it has done much to popularise ancient
drama, and the success of the National Theatre has had a great
influence on the Greek theatrical world in general. The North
of Greece State Theatre, for example, is also of a very high
standard. It gives regular winter performances in Salonica and
during summer presents mainly ancient drama at the open-air
theatre of Philippi, near Kavalla. It tours extensively in northern
Greece and also has a season in Athens.

With the exception of ancient drama, the number of Greek
plays presented by theatrical companies is meagre, largely because there are few of any consequence to produce. The Athenian theatre relies heavily on the works of foreign playwrights
and authors such as Ibsen and Tchekhov have always been
popular. At the same time, however, the more recent foreign
avant-garde plays also have had successful runs. Attendances
at the theatre follow a pattern similar to those of other countries
in that theatre-going varies substantially with financial status.
The Ekistics Survey indicated that 8.4 per cent of the population
of the eighteen communities studied visited the theatre at least
once in the preceding month. In reality the figures varied from
2.0 per cent for the low-income groups to 29.4 per cent for the
highest. Contemporary governments have imposed conditions
on the private sector to ensure that theatre-going falls within
the capacity of everyone's purse. It still remains largely a middle-
and upper-class activity.

MUSIC

With the exception of folksongs, Greece has no rich musical
tradition stretching back through the centuries. Any continuity

which did exist in the past came to an abrupt end when the Byzantine Empire fell to the Turks. On achieving independence Greece faced yet another dilemma, that of developing her own intellectual character in the arts. In music this has hardly been achieved, although certain names stand out as pioneers in the musical field.

Nicos Skalkotas (1904-49) is often regarded as the originator of the country's modern serious music. In 1948 the French Institute in Athens published the score of his *Four Greek Dances* for orchestra, which is possibly his best-known composition. More recent composers have reaped the benefits of his work and there now exists in Greece a school of modernists which includes Antiniou and Christou. Manolis Kalomiris has been another of the main representatives of serious music this century. Folk motifs and Byzantine melodies have strongly influenced his work, the latter being marked in his opera *Constantine Palaeolagos*. Undoubtedly the most famous contemporary Greek composer is Theodorakis, largely because of his political feelings and his more popular music such as *Zorba's Dance* and the score for the recent film *Z*. In the classical field, however, he has been acclaimed as one of the most important Greek composers of modern times. His burning patriotism has been harnessed to his musical ability, trained at the Paris Conservatoire. Theodorakis, following his release from a lengthy term as a political prisoner, now lives in exile. It is extremely unfortunate for Greece that at present his music is banned in the country that inspired his distinctive style.

The backbones of serious music today are the National Opera Company of Greece and the Athens State Orchestra. The National Opera first started work under State auspices in 1939 and it has built up a wide repertoire and produced a number of internationally known artists. The Athens State Orchestra is a much older institution. It was originally founded in 1893 but played under a variety of names until 1942 when it became a State organisation. In 1927 and 1928 its conductor was Dimitri Mitropoulos. The orchestra has done much in laying the foundations of Greece's musical life.

Popular Music

There is no denying the fact that Greek popular music has made a greater impact abroad than its serious variety. There are a number of reasons for this and much must be attributed to the successful 1960 film *Never on Sunday,* which served to highlight the fact that the Greeks had something new and fresh to offer the popular musical world. The score was by Manos Hadjidakis, another serious composer who has turned his creative ability to the infinitely more rewarding film and popular markets.

The music of Hadjidakis, Theodorakis, Xarhakos and others is essentially folk-song and folk-dance music with overtones of 'pop' music from abroad. It incorporates a variety of subtle influences, many of them stemming from the east and echoing the past history of the country. The music is tied mainly to love themes (tender, passionate, jealous) and also to grief, death and God, and emphasises the peasant background of modern Greece. It is colourful and vigorous and the dynamic sound comes from the *bouzouki,* an instrument brought to Greece by the refugees from Asia Minor in the 1920s. A decade ago the cult of the *bouzouki* was particularly strong in Greece and it still remains the most characteristic sound heard in the Athenian Plaka and in the taverns and restaurants of the Saronic coast. Male solo dancing or formation dancing to the Syrtaki form an integral part of the atmosphere of the *bouzoukia.* The smashing of wine glasses when fervour is high is now frowned upon by the government!

LITERATURE

As with music, the great literary heritage of Greece stops short in the fifteenth century. Throughout the long period of Turkish rule literature declined, and it was not until the nineteenth century that Greek poets and story-tellers were again heard.

In style nineteenth-century literature imitated that current in Western Europe and relied very little on earlier traditions. The great awakening in the country's modern literary development took place in the Ionian Islands, which had prospered materially and spiritually under Venetian and British rule. The intellectual renaissance was greatly advanced by the establishment of the Ionian Academy in Corfu during the governorship of Sir Frederick Adams. This attracted scholars from adjacent islands, and the Academy became the seat of a remarkable literary movement. The leaders were the poets Solomos and Mavilis and the critic Polylas.

Solomos (1798-1857), who came from Zante, has been regarded as the greatest 'modern' Greek poet. His principal works include *Hymn to Liberty, On the Death of Lord Byron, The Woman of Zante* and *The Cretan*, and much of it has been translated into English and French. Polylas (1826-96) was responsible for editing the works of Solomos and also for translating *The Iliad, The Odyssey* and the plays of Shakespeare into modern Greek.

The Ionian school were the leaders of the vigorous movement to establish vernacular Greek as a literary instrument for all purposes. Demotic champions included the poets Mavilis and Vlasto and the novelists Myribeles and Venezes. In 1888 John Psycharis acquired fame with the book *To Taxidi*, in which he took up the defence of the demotic tongue in a carefully worked out style. Other principal champions of the cause were Sikelianos, Palamas and Pallis, and publication of the latter's translation of *The Iliad* and the New Testament into demotic Greek provoked a violent riot in Athens on 8 November 1901.

George Serefis brought Greece its first Nobel Prize in 1963, and his noble poetic vision is continued in the works of Eythias, Gatsos, Matsas and Karouzos. Their even younger followers tend to combine ancient themes with modern experimental imagery. During the enemy occupation of World War II a school of clandestine and highly patriotic writers developed in Greece. Following the country's liberation they concentrated on works of detailed and aggressive social significance. A multiplicity of themes of consistent psychological depth appear in the novels of Sarantsis and Liberaki-Karapanu, and Prevelakis' work on Crete offers a startling new vision of the island.

Undoubtedly the most famous of Greece's contemporary authors was Nikos Katzantzakis (1883-1957). He was acclaimed by both Albert Schweitzer and Thomas Mann as one of the great writers of modern Europe. Katzantzakis devoted himself to the burning and passionate questions of philosophy and politics and from these experiences came his poetic credo, *The Saviour of God,* and his epic autobiography, *Report to Greco.* In Britain and the United States Katzantzakis is best known as the author of three enthusiastically acclaimed novels, *Zorba the Greek, Freedom from Death,* and *The Greek Passion.* Katzantzakis was also a dramatist, translator and travel writer. *The Odyssey: A Modern Sequel,* which he worked on over a period of twelve years, is considered to be his crowning achievement.

Many would now agree that Vassilis Vassilikos is the most promising writer of his generation. Born in Kavalla in 1933, he published his first novel at the age of twenty and in 1961 received the Award of the Group of Twelve for his trilogy of short novels, *The Plant, The Well, The Angel.* This award is given for the best fiction of the year and is the most respected literary prize in Greece. His current best-seller is his novel *Z* based on the murder of the Greek physician and parliamentarian Gregory Lambrakis. The film adaptation of *Z* by Jorge Semprun was France's official entry for the 1969 Cannes Film Festival, gaining the Jury Prize. The book is banned in Greece and Vassilikos is yet another Greek artist who has been forced into exile.

VISUAL ARTS

Much of the visual art of Greece is sadly confined to museums and archaeological sites. The great gulf between ancient and modern traditions is particularly wide in architecture. Greek cities are largely of modern creation and much of the urban architecture is of uninspiring contemporary design. It is perhaps

L

for this reason that the country's ancient ruins appear all the more majestic and noble when they exist in close proximity to modern structures. It is impossible to cover in a short section what people frequently call 'the perfection of Greek art,' yet a little must be said of the country's vestiges of the past if only because today they form one of the principal tourist attractions.

The three great ancient orders of architecture survive in the country's numerous ruined temples. The Doric order has long been regarded as the chief glory of Greek architecture. It evolved out of earlier traditions and is distinguishable by its columns, which were placed without any base on the upper foundations of buildings. A simple capital characterises Doric temples and their columns tapered upwards and generally had twenty flutings meeting each other at a sharp angle. Both the columns and the superstructure were originally constructed of wood, and many of their characteristic features, when later translated into stone, recall the original material. After 200 years of experimentation the Doric style reached its climax in the Parthenon, completed in 438BC and, with the exception of the wooden roof, built entirely of Pentelic marble.

The ancients called Doric the masculine order, and saw all the feminine graces in Ionic. The Ionic tradition first evolved across the Aegean in Asia Minor in the sixth century and gradually replaced the Doric style in the Greek mainland, though never completely, and there was much intermarriage between the two. Ionic columns differ in their elaborately moulded bases, slimmer shafts and a more decorative capital, the essential element being a small cushion whose sides curl in a spiral on either side of the shaft. On the Acropolis this order is well represented in the Erechtheion and the Temple of Nike, constructed during the last quarter of the fifth century. The Corinthian order is scarcely distinguishable from the Ionic except for its capital whose design consists, basically, of rows of leaf formations with central rosettes. It was in the buildings of the Roman period, for example the temple of Olympian Zeus in Athens, that the full possibilities of this decorative order were realised.

The long centuries of the Byzantine Empire left monuments

wholly different from those of classical Greece, but no less magnificent. To Greek simplicity were added Roman engineering skill and eastern opulence and from this fusion sprang an ornate architecture, frescoes and mosaics. Byzantine art witnessed three great periods of development between the sixth and fifteenth centuries and the evolution in form can be followed in the exquisite churches throughout Greece. With the exception of northern Greece, and particularly Salonica, Byzantine churches tend to be small, but the majority belonging to the later period take the standard shape of the Greek cross whose four equal arms served as a support for the dome. Small but fine examples dating from the eleventh century onwards can be seen in the old quarter of Athens, but perhaps one of the best examples of the Byzantine tradition in southern Greece is the eleventh-century church of Daphni, 5 miles from the centre of Athens. Its mosaics, though fragmentary, are rivalled only by those of the great basilicas of Salonica. On a broader canvas the ruined Byzantine town of Mistra in the Peloponnesus, the monastic republic of Mount Athos, Salonica, and the Byzantine Museum, Athens, are rich areas for the study of the art form of this period.

Crusader and Venetian architecture is common in many parts of Greece, but the Turks, in the course of three and a half centuries, constructed few important monuments, and what they did accomplish was systematically effaced by the Greeks on independence. In nineteenth-century Athens the classical tradition was reintroduced in a number of public buildings, the most famous group located in University Street. The University itself, built in 1839-42 by the Danish architect Christian Hansen, has a handsome Ionic portico in Pentelic marble and is regarded as the least disturbing of the group which also includes the National Library and the Hellenic Academy. An interesting building, the eye hospital, also located in University Street, was built along traditional Byzantine lines, but this influence has been most prominent in ecclesiastical architecture, whose form and arrangement still follows closely that of earlier churches.

In the fine arts Greece witnessed two awakenings in the period from the fall of Constantinople to Greek independence. Both came in areas which were free from Turkish domination. In Crete there was a late renaissance of Byzantine art in the sixteenth century, resulting in the fresco paintings of many Cretan churches. Crete produced the distinguished name of Domenico Theotocopoulous whom Spain and the world still honour as El Greco. When the island fell to the Turks, Cretan painters left for the continent, Mount Athos and the Ionian Islands. Many settled in Zante after 1669, before moving to Corfu where they played an important part in the Ionian cultural revival. These periods, however, during which painting flourished, were brief, and because of their regional character few national traditions have developed. Modern art undoubtedly owes much to the influence of El Greco, but he must be regarded as a European rather than an essentially Greek painter.

Today Greece has many contemporary artists and thriving colonies are to be found throughout the islands. The fact is, however, that the country is not really rich enough to support artists and many are dependent on the sale of their work to summer visitors. Also, the country has few permanent picture galleries and most work is exhibited privately and, if the opportunity arises, in exhibitions abroad. The latter, of course, often requires government or private sponsorship. The awarding of the Unesco Prize at the 1960 Venice Biennale to the painter Yannis Spyropoulos may be taken as a sign that Greek art is now on the upgrade and many artists have held frequent shows abroad in the last decade. Greece has its own pavilion at the Biennale, but nationally the most important exhibition is the Panhellenic Exposition of Pictorial Art, held every two years.

THE PRESS

The Greeks are voracious newspaper readers, which provides them with the necessary ammunition for conversation and debate in the cafés and coffee houses. It has been estimated that one out of every ten Greeks buys a newspaper each day and in Athens and Salonica alone over 700,000 papers are sold daily. Around 114 daily newspapers circulate in Greece, of which 26 are published in Athens and Salonica. There are a further 70 local, mainly weekly newspapers, about 300 papers other than dailies published in Athens, and more than 500 periodicals.

The government exercises strong control on the press and special laws regulate the publication and operations of newspapers. Newsprint is obtained from the State free of duty, but its supply is controlled to limit the circulation of selected newspapers. The problem of censorship and the closing down of a number of newspapers after 1967 has already been mentioned. Prior to the present government's term in office the Athens area had a choice between a large number of influential newspapers, the most important of which were *Nea* (circulation 147,000), *Messimvrini* (54,000), *Vima* (44,000), *Akropolis* (33,000) and *Kathimerini* (30,000). An interesting development has been the substantial increase in circulation (10,000 to 60,000) of the pro-revolution paper *Eleftheros Kosmos,* though this, too, mildly criticises government policy. Today the conservative paper *Akropolis* is Greece's oldest remaining daily.

Foreign newspapers are readily available in Athens and Salonica, and Athens also publishes the daily English language papers, *Athens News* and *Athens Daily Post* and the French *Le Messager d'Athenes.* The two most important periodicals are *Gynaiki* (Woman) and *Ikones* (Pictures) and in 1965, within the Athens area alone, these had a circulation of 110,000 and 60,000 respectively.

SPORT

The first modern Olympic Games were held in Athens in 1896. The Panathenaic Stadium had been completely restored a year earlier at the expense of George Averoff, a wealthy Alexandrian Greek. Since this time the all-marble stadium, with a capacity of 70,000, has been the scene of numerous sporting events and international contests. It witnessed the closing ceremony of the 1969 European Athletic Championships and also the arrival of the marathon race. For all other events Greece broke with tradition and used the newly completed Karaiskaki Stadium at New Phaleron. The faultless organisation of the 1969 Games and the modern facilities at New Phaleron are indicative of Greece's interest in sporting events.

With the active encouragement of the government the General Secretariat for Sport is directing all its efforts to extend sporting facilities throughout the country. In recent years forty-five modern stadiums have been built and over a thousand municipal and communal sports grounds improved. Large sums have been spent on equipment to aid the organisation of athletic events on a national and international level.

Most of the better-known sports are now practised in Greece and are fast gaining enthusiasts. Football, in particular, is extremely popular, and most Greek centres have their local soccer teams with widespread spectator interest. In Athens the three largest stadiums are the Panathenaikos (capacity 25,000), the AEK (35,000) and the Karaiskaki (45,000). Motor racing has gained in popularity in recent years and important national and international events are organised. The Acropolis Rally attracts many foreign drivers, but keen local interest has helped to develop the Autumn Rally, the Boeotia-Attica Rally and a number of other events. Speed racing is held on circuits at Rhodes, Corfu, Canea, Tatoi, etc, and mountain climbing tests, greatly aided by the improvement to the country's roads, attract many spectators. Water sports show a concentration at Phaleron Bay, where the Royal Yacht Club is located and the Aegean and Ionian yacht races are popular annual events with many foreign competitors. Rowing regattas are held during the summer months at Poros and Ioannina.

Mountain climbing and hiking are fast-developing activities, and since the war they have been organised under a number of national associations and clubs. Winter sports have developed more slowly, but a number of ski-ing centres are located throughout the country, the largest at Metsoven on the borders of Epirus and Thessaly.

9

Hints for Visitors

The choice of season for travelling in Greece depends entirely on the individual. Summer, of course, attracts most visitors from abroad, but it is worth adding that Greece can be enjoyed at all seasons, even winter, when many areas experience long spells of sunny weather. Greece tends to be at its best for foreign visitors in spring and autumn, which can be considered as prolonged and cooler editions of summer. Moreover, hotels are less crowded during these seasons. Summer, which begins early in May, goes on relentlessly until September, and in July and August the heat is considerable. But although hot, summer is rendered bearable by the dryness of the atmosphere, and on the coasts by the etesian winds.

Greece can still be regarded as one of the cheapest countries in Europe, especially for visitors arriving from the United States and Western Europe. Like all countries, of course, it depends on the habits and needs of the individual, and those accustomed to luxury-class hotels, expensive drinks and night-clubs etc will have to pay accordingly. Even so, hotel prices are lower than those charged by the corresponding class of establishment in the United States and in most European countries. Hotels are classified into luxury (L), first class (A), second class (B), third class (C), fourth class (D), and fifth class (E) establishments, and maximum and minimum hotel prices per room are fixed by law for each season. The prices quoted by hotels should therefore include all lawful extras and moreover they are subject to a number of rebates in favour of the visitor. A 20 per cent reduction on the price of each room is allowed for foreign guests and for Greeks permanently resident abroad. During the winter season, which for accommodation purposes extends from 1 November to 30 March, prices are compulsorily reduced by 10 per cent and can be voluntarily reduced by up to 30 per cent. Hotel capacity has increased considerably in recent years, but nevertheless, at the height of the summer season and particularly in the main tourist centres it is advisable to reserve accommodation well in advance. If difficulties should arise the help of the tourist police is often invaluable.

Apart from hotels, Greece offers the visitor other forms of accommodation. There has been a substantial increase in the number of well-equipped motels built for a capacity of 30 to 50 vehicles and 60 to 100 beds. At several of the summer resorts there are also tourist villages with the necessary comforts and conveniences. In regions without hotels, and especially in the islands, accommodation can be found in private houses, where the hospitality of the host makes up for the modest accommodation. In selected villages this custom has been organised by the Royal National Foundation to ensure reasonable standards of comfort and cleanliness. Monasteries, too, usually have separate quarters where visitors can stay, and one is expected to leave some money in the alms-box. For the monastic community of Mount Athos the visitor, who must be male and (unless a theological student) over twenty-one years of age, is required to apply through his consul to the Foreign Ministry in Athens or to the Minister for Northern Greece in Salonica for a permit to visit Athos. The document must be presented immediately upon arrival to the Nomarch of Karyes, who will issue a residence permit, usually for ten to fifteen days, which has to be presented at each monastery visited.

Camping is legal throughout Greece, but as yet there are few specially indicated camping grounds. The Greek Automobile and Touring Club (ELPA) and the Hellenic Touring Club (EPL) are introducing a chain of camping sites for caravans and tents in various parts of the country with a view to attracting Western Europe's peripatetic holiday-makers. The Greek Youth Hostel

Association (4, Odhos Dragatsaniou, Athens) is affiliated to the International Youth Hostels Federation. There are hostels in Athens, Patras, Iraklion, Rhodes, Delphi, Ioannina, Salonica, Syra, Myconos and Corfu as well as smaller ones elsewhere. The quality of accommodation varies considerably and many are not to be recommended. Hostels are also open to students in some of the larger centres.

All information regarding motoring in Greece can be obtained from the ELPA office at 6 Amerikis St, Athens, 134. Road traffic keeps to the right and the speed limit in built-up areas varies according to the nature of the roads and other conditions of circulation. Normally it is 30 miles an hour, but this may be decreased (or increased) by local authorities. In an attempt to speed up traffic circulation in central Athens, all vehicles must at all times keep up a speed of 25 miles an hour. It may not be out of place to warn foreign visitors to exercise extreme caution when driving in Greece. The virtuosity of Greek drivers is sometimes truly astonishing, and driving in Athens is certainly not a sedative to the nerves. Good and up-to-date road maps are published under the aegis of the ELPA, which also has regional offices in Salonica, Larisa, Volos, Patras, Canea and Corfu.

Many visitors are attracted to Greece solely on account of its rich archaeological and historical remains. A wealth of museums and ancient sites is found all over the country, but it is possible to obtain a good idea of the country's history by making Athens the principal base. The hours during which museums and archaeological sites are open to the public vary according to the season, and entrance fees range from 5 to 20drs according to location and to the importance of the remains. A day's tour of the museums and ancient sites of Athens can prove quite expensive, and it is useful to bear in mind that admission is free every Thursday and Sunday. On all other days university students are admitted at half the entrance fees, and all teachers and students of foreign schools of archaeology, art and architecture can obtain a pass card from the Archaeological Resources Fund, 1 Tossizza St, Athens. Photography in museums and archaeological sites is permitted provided a light camera without a tripod is used. The purchase of antiquities and historical relics, except from an authorised dealer, is forbidden, and even then a special licence is necessary from the General Directorate of Antiquities in order to take purchases out of the country.

The country's popular arts and crafts make some of the best souvenirs of a visit to Greece. A tradition handed down through the centuries has resulted in regional specialisation in certain handicraft products. The region of Ioannina produces silverware and ornaments of an original style (known as *Yanniotika*) and Rhodes also produces gold and silverware (*Rhoditika*) and a wide range of pottery. Kalamata is famous for its silks, Kastoria for its fur-trimming trade, Myconos for its weaving and embroidery and Vytina for its wood carving. The National Handicrafts Organisation maintains permanent showrooms in Athens.

The Greek language can be something of a problem to the visitor, although English, French and German are widely understood in Athens and in all large hotels and tourist offices. It is outside the cities that the major difficulties in communication are encountered, and the visitor is advised to be familiar at least with the Greek alphabet. This is indispensable for reading street and bus signs, and the foreigner will be astounded by the large number of Greek words which have almost their exact equivalent in English. Any attempt on the part of the visitor to speak the native language is warmly appreciated by the Greeks.

Tipping is expected for most services rendered. A 15 per cent service charge is generally included in hotel bills, but it is customary for the client to give an additional small tip to any of the personnel who have served him with particular care. Such tips range from 20 to 50 drachmas. In restaurants, cafés, bars, night clubs, etc service is included in the bill, but again it is the custom to leave an additional 3 to 5 drachmas per person served for the waiter, and 2 to 3 drachmas for his assistant. The waiter's tip is left on the plate and the assistant's on the table. Taxi-drivers do not generally expect a tip, but one seldom takes back the odd drachma when paying the fare.

The goodwill to render a service or help a foreign visitor in any manner possible is characteristic of the Greeks generally.

Xenios Zeus, the god of hospitality, is very much alive, and on the islands in particular the almost instinctive quality of the hospitality can be overwhelming. Nevertheless there are some country districts where strangers are avoided and others where the mass influx of tourists has broken down the intimate contact that once existed between villager and visitor.

Acknowledgements

I wish to express my thanks to the Bank of Greece and the Greek National Tourist Organisation for their help in the preparation of this book. To the secretarial and technical staff of the Department of Geography, University of Strathclyde, I am indebted for assistance in the final presentation of the manuscript.

Index